A Life to Dai For

A Life to Dai For
Dai Jones Llanilar

with Lyn Ebenezer

The publishers wish to acknowledge the support of
Cyngor Llyfrau Cymru

Cover photograph: Arvid Parry-Jones
Cover design: Y Lolfa

ISBN: 978 1 78461 447 8

Published and printed in Wales
on paper from well-maintained forests by
Y Lolfa Cyf., Talybont, Ceredigion SY24 5HE
website www.ylolfa.com
e-mail ylolfa@ylolfa.com
tel 01970 832 304
fax 832 782

Contents

1

What's new?

TWENTY YEARS HAVE flown by since my first Welsh-language autobiography was published. It is 13 years since the English translation *Dai and Let Live* appeared. What has passed during those latter years is now water under the bridge. And billions of gallons of the Ystwyth river have flowed into Cardigan Bay during that time. They have been, in general, two happy decades. One of the very few negatives is the fact that I am now 20 years older and, as a result of those passing years, not as sprightly as I used to be. Not that I was ever very agile. My shepherd's crook has always been a support rather than an ornament. Mind you, my ever-expanding paunch has much to answer for that.

As far as work and life in general is concerned, things have not changed all that much during the two decades. Indeed, life is much as it was. But within the larger picture there have been obvious changes. New faces and new activities have joined or replaced the old. Some of those vanished faces and events, alas, I will never see again. But the world is largely unchanged. My small world at least.

Here in the Ystwyth valley the situation remains largely

the same for Olwen and I at Berthlwyd Farm, other than the fact that our son John now shoulders most of the work, helped by his partner Laura. Olwen, as usual, does more than her share, while I largely observe. You could, perhaps, describe me as a gentleman farmer. Somebody once described a gentleman farmer as someone who raises nothing on his land except his cap. I don't even raise that. But I do still raise cattle and sheep, as well as cobs these days.

The most significant development family-wise is that Olwen and I have become grandparents. Yes, there is a continuation, a family succession. And to those of us who live off the land, continuation and succession is important. We have two granddaughters. The elder is now 19 and already drives a car. The other is five and drives us potty with her mischief-making and innocent naughtiness. Celine lives in Llanddewibrefi and has begun her college studies. Her ambition is to teach nursery children. Ella is here with us.

Yes, being grandparents has been one of the greatest events of the past 20 years. It is wonderful having them both around the place. The actor and comedian W.C. Fields once said that one should never work with children and animals. Well, I'm more than happy to work with both groups, children and animals. Apart from cats, that is. And the grandchildren have transformed my life completely. It is strange having someone as young as Ella around the place, with her endless questioning. Every chance she gets she interrogates me with the intensity of a prosecuting barrister.

Children want to know everything. They are inquisitive by nature. It is a part of their make-up. But one has to be careful what one says when answering. Children will inevitably repeat everything they hear to their friends and teachers at school the following day. And Ella is totally different from what I was like when I was her age. I would be reluctant to go to school. I had to be practically dragged there. But she loves school. Children can change one's life completely. Or is it that they change one's attitude to life? Both, possibly.

Yes, Ella loves school. I am a firm believer in doing everything possible to keep small rural schools open. This has a lot to do with the fact that I myself was educated at a small village school. Llangwyryfon school, or 'Llangwrddon' to any true native, remains open. It was there, despite my reluctance to attend, that an attempt was made to enlighten me, a thoroughbred village idiot. Some aspects, such as playtimes, were fine. And due to persistent persuasion by patient teachers such as headmistress Mrs Andrews, I did leave somewhat more knowledgeable than when I had started.

Later, at Dinas Secondary Modern School in Aberystwyth, a different kind of educational persuasion was adopted that involved drumming some sense into my uncultured brain. The day that I was released from Dinas school for the last time was the happiest day of my life.

My five years there had taught me nothing except how best to avoid upsetting the Social Science teacher, Mair Evans, who was not a woman to be crossed.

I am now 73 and still battling on. The days of my childhood and my youth seem like only yesterday. At Dinas school I remember Tegwyn Rhosgoch, another fellow sufferer, having to write 'lines' as punishment for some misdemeanour or other. This happened regularly. Just as regularly Tegwyn, somehow or other, would always manage to avoid this pointless mode of punishment. A few years after he left school, he chanced upon the Welsh teacher, W.R. Edwards, on the street in Aberystwyth.

'Well! Well! Mr Edwards!' said Tegwyn. 'You're still alive! Damn, you must be at least a hundred!'

Edwards, bless him, merely laughed. At Dinas school we, country children, were always derided by many of the teachers and especially by the 'townie' pupils. We were the uncivilised rabble from the bush. But, more often that not, *we* would have the last word.

Looking back, I realise that being taught at Llangwrddon school was a privilege. And, as noted, this has made me realise the importance of retaining our village schools. One of the happiest sounds anyone can hear is that of children out playing on the school yard. I was filming in Aberdaron a while ago and the Crud y Werin school children were out at play. Incidentally, what an appropriate name for a place of learning. Crud y Werin means Cradle of the Common Folk.

The village school is, indeed, the educational cradle for the locality. The school is the gurgling, bubbling wellspring of the neighbourhood. Once a village school closes, there is no reopening. That closure is final.

I travel extensively and nothing saddens me more than seeing an empty school, its windows boarded up. Some are already dilapidated. A village without its school is like a cemetery. Silence reigns. Some, it is true, have been adapted into community centres. Fine, but not at the expense of the local school – but better than seeing a school or chapel turned into a carpet store. Occasionally, a closed school or chapel adapted as a community centre will contribute something to village life. I was in Pennal not so very long ago attending the funeral of Menna, the widow of my old friend and hero Richard Rees. The chapel there is now a community hall. At least the locals will reap some benefits from it.

Not only are village schools beneficial; headteachers and teachers themselves can also be influential beyond the precincts of their schools. Here in Llanilar we were most fortunate in having amongst us as headmaster in the 1960s J.R. Evans, a prominent dramatist. And after J.R. we had Beti Griffiths, who was at the heart of all local activities. They both belonged to an era when headteachers and teachers were pillars of the community and lived locally. Today, headteachers are swamped with paperwork. They have little time for teaching, let alone being central to local activities. In addition, we have headteachers nowadays who are in charge of two, three or even four schools within a ten- or twenty-mile radius. Headteachers are administrators rather than educationalists in this day and age.

As well as being a dramatist, J.R. Evans also served as a local magistrate, as did Beti after him. One day a local man appeared in front of J.R. charged with poaching. He had been caught naked, wrestling with a salmon in a pool in the Ystwyth river. When asked the reason for his naked presence in the river Ystwyth in the early hours of the morning, he replied, 'Perhaps it is the Ystwyth river to you, sir. But to me it is more like the Ganges. The fish had been contaminated by the impure water and I merely jumped in to save it.'

That was his explanation for being naked in the Ystwyth river at five o'clock in the morning. How J.R. loved that!

Unfortunately, school and chapel closures in our villages are but a part of the decline in the standard of country life. Shops and banks are closing too. Young people are leaving for the cities in droves. Local activities are few and far between. Here in Llanilar, on the first Friday of every November, Carmel chapel would be packed to the rafters for the village agricultural show concert. There would be an audience of over 500 people appreciating some of Wales' top talents. Not any more. And that is but one example: the annual Good Friday eisteddfod now belongs to the past as well. I could go on and on.

Despite all this, some things remain unchanged. Here at Berthlwyd we still raise Welsh Black cattle and native Welsh sheep or half-Welsh and cross-breeds on our 300 acres. The Welsh Black has lost much of its popularity. Indeed, this is a period that is as black for the breed's future as the cattle themselves. The Dolgellau market reflects that decline. Not so long ago it would be a two-day event. Today you will be lucky to see a dozen or two Welsh Blacks there. The breed needs to be marketed with more positive publicity. The Welsh Black is a special species, one of our few surviving native breeds.

The breed has been ousted by continental cattle that react better to concentrated feed. There was a time when the Welsh Black was to be seen on practically every farm in Wales. And it is a fine breed. She nurtures her offspring without any trouble, while the continental breeds lack milk while raising their young.

By now, however, we have had to conform too, and have bought a white Charolais bull for cross-breeding with our herd. This was John's idea based solely on the market. Their offspring are worth so much more.

How different the situation is regarding Welsh cobs. They are now to be found worldwide. The cob to me is the perfect symbol to represent Wales. Seeing cob stallions strutting around the main ring at a show, raising their hooves gracefully, is a sight that once seen is never forgotten.

What has really changed with us at Berthlwyd is that we have adopted agricultural contracting to a far greater extent. This is John's expertise and he employs two or three helpers. A farmer has to diversify today or stagnate. He or she has no choice. The main difference between John and myself is that he is a four-wheel man while I have more faith in four legs. John veers towards the mechanical; I am a cattle, sheep, horse and sheepdog man. Despite that difference we get on well together.

Ageing brings with it its own problems. Previously, after returning from filming I would, after a cup of tea, change immediately into my working clothes. Nowadays I tend to take things easier and wait till the following morning. But I am determined not to loosen my grip on things. Once you become a farmer, there is no escape. It runs in your blood. It becomes an innate part of your very being and lasts for life. Farming is embedded in my flesh and runs through my bone marrow.

When people greet me nowadays they often do so by asking the age-old question, 'How are you?' I will usually answer, 'I feel rather tired. I've been busy lately.' And then comes the inevitable retort, 'Dai bach, there's an answer to that. Why don't you retire? It's high time you did.'

But it's easier said than done. I don't believe I could ever retire. And so I still carry on farming. And I still carry on filming and broadcasting, travelling the country from one end to the other and often abroad as well.

The Good Lord has been more than kind to me. For one thing, he has given me good health. I am as healthy now as I have ever been, apart from diabetes which is under control. It is far more important to have good health than a healthy bank balance in this old world. And the chance to enjoy it. In fact, if enjoyment was money, then I would be a millionaire.

Within the wider context, things have changed a little – not only here on the farm but in my media work as well. These changes may not be so evident to others. For instance, once upon a time we would be six or seven as a film crew out on location. There would be the cameraman and camera assistant, a lighting technician, a sound man and assistant, the producer and the producer's assistant. And myself, of course. Sometimes I could swear that, when we would all be assembled on some farmyard or other, there would be more cars than crew members. Today we are down to half that number. Four of us will now turn up in two cars. The biggest change, I suppose, is that I now double up as producer as well as presenter. This is referred to today as multitasking, a word that is as difficult to pronounce as it is to spell.

The advantage of working on my TV programme *Cefn Gwlad* (The Countryside) from the very beginning is that I have always been a farmer too. I know by instinct the likes and dislikes of my fellow farmers. I know their taste. And when I interview another farmer I have to remember the importance of not upsetting him or her. I need to keep them happy enough to fill 30 minutes of film. The last thing I want is for the farmer to be unnerved by something before we finish filming.

During the early years, *Cefn Gwlad* meant filming 22 programmes annually. It involved – and still does – far more that one day's filming per programme. I am also involved in the research made prior to the shoot. Following the filming and editing, I am called down to the studio in Cardiff to record voice-overs. This involves dubbing up to four programmes per day. So much work means that a year can fly by.

For some time, the crew has been driving around in an official *Cefn Gwlad* car provided by car dealer David Gravell of Kidwelly, a gesture that we greatly appreciate. It means a considerable reduction in mileage for my own car. During the early years, when I was still much involved with my singing career, I would travel over 100,000 miles each year. I would leave the house early, often straight after pre-dawn milking, and not be home much before first light the next morning. The television work that came later meant returning home just in time for the evening's milking. The old car would not have much time to breathe! It was always on the road.

I don't like driving. Often I have no choice. But it is much preferable to be chauffeured now and then. And I will here reveal a secret – I am terrible at reversing, especially when reversing a trailer. I often become the centre of attention at Tregaron mart when I try to reverse. In fact, my reversing is by now so legendary that I seem to attract a crowd of onlookers. Indeed, such is the interest that I create that I should be awarded a grant by the Arts Council for my creativity. Honestly, many acts have received grants for much less original entertainment!

Some of you from among my generation will remember a public information clip that used to be shown on television in the 1960s. It involved a hopeless driver that, like me, found reversing almost impossible. He was known as Reginald Molehusband, and was married with two children. His parking was regarded as a threat to public safety. People came from miles around just to see Reginald attempt to park his car. Bets were placed on his performance. Whatever Reginald missed while reversing he was sure to collide with later. Bus and taxi drivers would change their routes just to avoid him... until the day that Reginald did it right! I still remember the commentary:

'Not too close, far enough forward... come on Reggie... and reverse in slowly... come on... and watching traffic... and park perfectly! Well done Reginald Molehusband, the safest parker in town.'

Then, all those watching would applaud. Unfortunately, only the first part of the information clip applied to me. Often at marts a kind bystander will offer to take my place behind the steering wheel. And I will gladly accept. Driving to me, and especially reversing, is a nuisance. But as I have to drive so much, it is a necessary nuisance.

I was somewhat clumsy as a child. And I would attribute my clumsiness to what I believed was my defective eyesight. Not so long ago I visited an optician in Aberystwyth and asked him for an eye test. The optician, Clive Williams, assured me that my eyesight was fine. I explained to him that when I was a schoolboy in Llangwrddon my headmistress,

Mrs Andrews, decided that I suffered with what is still known as a 'lazy eye' in my right eye. I explained to Clive that when I checked the car mirror when reversing I had to close one eye. Clive's abrupt answer was, 'Perhaps it's your nose getting in the way!'

Over the past 20 years my reversing has not improved one bit. But, as I have already noted, there have been other changes. The media work still remains highly pleasurable. These days it takes up three days per week, leaving me with four days of being involved with the farm. And I spend every Friday morning recording my weekly Sunday night radio programme *Ar Eich Cais* (At Your Request) at the BBC studio in Aberystwyth. This gives me as much pleasure as anything I do.

Things have got easier over the years. It's a matter of getting used to things, to become used to the routine. Throughout my television and radio career I have never been dependent on others for my scripts. I enjoy preparing my own and doing so at leisure. It means that the words I utter are my own and, as such, they are easy to recall in front of the camera. Not that I have ever been a slave to my script, no more than I was ever tied to singing from a copy. Everything I do is off-the-cuff and from the heart. Scripts and music copies are merely guides to me.

Occasionally, I visit London where I was born a Welsh-speaking Cockney. Last year I had the opportunity to visit Castle Street chapel where I addressed one of the Saturday Afternoon Society's monthly gatherings. The minister of the

Welsh Church of Central London is a prominent musician who used to be S4C's head of music, Robert Nicholls from Penclawdd. From the outset, Rob was determined to bring worshippers of the various London Welsh congregations together. I was honoured to address their very first meeting.

Castle Street chapel is where my family worshipped, my grandparents and parents among them. I attended Sunday school there until my voluntary exile to Wales to live with Uncle Morgan and Aunty Hannah. Every time I returned to London on holiday or during weekend visits I would attend the chapel with my parents. The minister when I was a child was Walter P. John from Pontarddulais. He was an eloquent preacher and had a very expressive voice. Among the regular worshippers was the musician and composer Dr Terry James. Castle Street was where Lloyd George worshipped. Another faithful member was Lewis Lewis of Llanrhystud. He was a deacon and grew a distinguished beard and looked like an Old Testament prophet.

My relationship with London has always been ambiguous. As a child I would long to live in the countryside. One of the attractions was the thought of having my own sheepdog. I had been given a book featuring a sheepdog called Black Bob, and I longed to live on a farm and own a sheepdog like Bob. Yet when I moved to live with my uncle and aunt, my thoughts often turned to London and my parents. Every Friday evening Uncle Morgan and Aunty Hannah would take me to the red phone kiosk in Llangwrddon so that I could ring home. I still remember my parents' phone number. It was Archway 5006. Really, it wasn't difficult to choose where I wanted to live. The city boy was now a country boy through and through.

When I went to Castle Street to address the Saturday Afternoon Society the place was packed. The audience included many exiles from the Llangwrddon area, among them Tom and Leis Lloyd. Leis, known as Leis Cornel, had been one of my childhood friends. She and Tom had been driven to the meeting by their son Ifan. Tom and Leis had kept a shop, The Candy Bar, 555 Holloway Road, for decades. Their presence at the meeting was a great comfort as they faced me from the front row. Later, of course, we talked of the old days in Llangwrddon over a cup of tea. Leis commented: 'I can't believe that we have met again under such circumstances, and you having been such a mischievous child!'

Leis made me feel at home. And I remembered our weekly journey to Sunday school together. We would be driven there by Evans Tanglogau in his old Ford car. With him up front would be William Howells, Pant-teg. Squashed in the back seat like sardines in a tin would be Olwen Maesbeidiog, my brother Trefor and myself. And taking up most of the remaining space would be Leis. The old car would just about make it to the summit of Pengelli Hill. Indeed, should Leis Cornel have happened to bring her handbag with her, the Ford's engine would have stuttered and stalled and we would all have had to get out and push!

How great it was to meet up with Leis once more. The memories came flooding back. And yes, Leis had brought her handbag along with her, tucked securely beneath her arm.

2

Roots

As I noted in *Dai and Let Live*, Llangwrddon is located at the bottom of a valley shaped like a natural bowl. Whichever direction you take when you leave the village, it means a climb. It is as if the village does its best to stop you from leaving. All the hills have names. There is Vicarage Hill, Chapel Hill, Tanrallt Hill and Carnau Hill, 'carnau' meaning hooves. Carnau Hill's name originates from a time when horses not only worked the land but were also the only mode of transport. Hence, the sound of hooves would be heard regularly.

This area of Ceredigion (the county was known as Cardiganshire until 1974) was – and remains – cob country, and members of my family have been involved with cobs for generations. Brynchwith, where my grandparents John and Mari Jones lived, was famous for its cobs. There my grandparents raised ten children, my father among them. I would call regularly as a child and would play with my four cousins, Islwyn, Trefor, Ceredig and Mair.

One of my uncles, Uncle Dan, owned a famous cob mare, Wyre Star. The river Wyre runs through the area. In fact there are two, the Lesser Wyre and the Great Wyre. They join to form one river that empties into Cardigan Bay. Wyre was therefore an apt prefix for Uncle Dan's cobs. Over the years the interest in breeding cobs had largely vanished among my family, until I recently began keeping a few at Berthlwyd.

One reason for my previous reluctance in keeping cobs was the need, when showing, to run alongside them at various shows. Running has never appealed to me. I wasn't built for speed. The only part of my body ever to run has been my nose. Running on two legs is anathema to me. There has been only one exception. By some unexplained miracle, I won the right to represent Dinas school at the schools' County Sports. I still find it difficult to believe that I ever won a race. In fact, I would find it difficult to win a three-legged race even if I grew a third leg.

I have, however, animals that can run and frolic. They are cobs which came from the Ilar Stud originally. I have sold some of my cob mares to local breeders, enthusiasts like Ceri Drefaes who is one of my neighbours. He has a granddaughter and I gave him a colt to present to her after her birth. Ceri does a good job with the cobs. He hails from the Brynele family of Bwlchllan. That in itself means that he is a horseman through and through.

I have so many cobs these days that I will have to do something about it. If I carry on like this I'll have more cobs than I have cows. Among them at the moment are two young fillies and a breeding mare. There is nothing that compares with keeping cobs. Imagine waking up in the morning, looking out through the bedroom window and seeing a mare and its foal in the field. What a scene! There exists a very special relationship between a mare and its foal. The same is true of Welsh Black cattle. Imagine seeing the first-born calf of the year. It is just like seeing the first newborn lamb of the year. This is one of the joys of farming, witnessing succession at work.

Things are very different in the mechanical world. In that particular sphere I am totally ignorant. Not that it should surprise anyone. I could never cherish something mechanical, something devoid of a soul. An animal has a soul. It has a spirit, especially the cob.

One example of today's modern technology that leaves me cold is the mobile phone. Such contraptions are a plague to me. I am totally bewildered by them. For one thing my fingertips are far too large to operate them. Whenever I attempt to press a button, I inevitably press two. I now have a mobile phone that has the largest buttons available, almost the size of tombstones. But to no avail. Modern phones offer all sorts of things, texting, taking photographs, perusing the internet. Before long you will be able to use your mobile to boil an egg! They offer you every service possible except the ease of the service I desire most of all, simply phoning someone.

No, I have no mechanical or technological ability. Driving my car is my mechanical limit. But, as I have noted, I have no choice but to drive. Today, unfortunately, a mobile phone is just as essential as a car, especially to someone like me who is often filming in remote areas.

When I started fronting the horse trotting TV series *Rasus* (Races) some 20 years ago on S4C, I was offered a mobile phone by one of the directors, John Watkin, who lives in Ffair Rhos. I accepted his kind offer immediately and he showed me a boxful of phones. He invited me to pick the handset of my choice. It was exactly like choosing a sweet from a box of Milk Tray. I plunged my hand in, just as if I was taking part in the lucky dip attraction at a chapel bazaar, and picked one out at random. A few days later I had occasion to send a text. There I was, shouting my message into the damn phone. Nothing happened. There was no response from the handset. I was talking to myself. I didn't realise I had to type my message.

One problem is having to remember my own mobile number. The only way out was for me to stick a piece of paper on the back of the phone and write my number down on that. I have owned my present phone for almost 20 years and I am none the wiser and cannot remember my number without checking the piece of paper on the back. I can just about manage to answer a call when the handset rings. But nothing more intricate than that.

One day I was at the Talbot Hotel in Tregaron when I was summoned by the barman. He told me John Watkin had left a message asking me to ring him. Out came the handset. I pressed the appropriate keys. Nothing happened. In the end I had to leave the bar and cross the road to use the red kiosk outside the Memorial Hall. Thank goodness that some of them still remain. The biggest problem is finding one that hasn't been vandalised.

However, I do have an aversion to red phone boxes. When I was a child a gang of us local kids would play around the kiosk on the village square in Llangwrddon. One of our games involved catching cats and trapping them inside the kiosk. The cats would go berserk, screeching and spitting. It was one game that I avoided like the plague. I would much rather face a bear than a cat. Trefor Maesbeidiog was to blame for my terror of moggies. One day, when I was ill, he and his sister Olwen called to see me. He had picked up a kitten somewhere along the way and had hidden it beneath his coat. Suddenly, without warning, he threw it on my bed. The enraged creature jumped at me and dug its claws into me. I grabbed it and threw it out of the window, but not before it had left its calling card on the blankets. From that day on I have not been able to be within a mile of a cat. Every time I see one I freeze. I stand petrified. I now know what Lot's wife went through.

I have come to realise how much I use Biblical analogy. It all harks back to Sunday school and the weekly 'seiat', which was an evening fellowship meeting. In my day these were just as important as attending school. As children we would attend without question; they were an integral part of our education. I am not romanticising for bygone things. But as I grow older I become aware of my dependence on Biblical and hymnal phrases. I think this is true of all of us country people of my age and beyond. Often a Biblical verse or a line of a hymn comes to mind. Our debt to the Christian religion is immeasurable. And yes, I know I should begin attending chapel again.

It's hard to believe how faithful I used to be to the local chapel. I would attend three times every Sunday. After moving to Llanilar I would always attend the Sunday morning service. The same was true every time I visited my parents in London, as I have already noted. Nowadays I seldom attend. One reason is my frequent absences from home. Having been away filming, sometimes for days, I spend weekends catching up with farm duties. I do, however, feel guilt about this and I am determined to try and attend regularly once more.

One pleasure as I get older, when I get a minute's peace, is to retire quietly to the parlour now and again to contemplate and meditate on times gone by. More often than not this involves looking at my trophies that are arrayed, row upon row, in a glass cabinet. These ribbands, medals and cups remind me of many a success at eisteddfods, agricultural shows and sheepdog trials. Not that I gloat over them. No, I contemplate them with pride and with nostalgia. I have no television set in the parlour, so I can sit back without any distractions and recall where I was and how I won them. I just sit there looking at them, musing. Every single one has its own story. And it's not so much the delight of reminiscing about my successes. More pleasant is the memory of taking part in competitions among dear old friends. Back in those days even losing would be a pleasure. I recall, among the adjudicators for example, that great character E.D. Jones, Tregaron, or 'Jonesy Bach' as he was universally known.

Another pleasure for me these days is frequenting the sheep mart in Tregaron on Fridays, or going to Welshpool mart on Mondays, and sometimes Dolgellau mart when I need to sell some of my Welsh Blacks. And it's better still if I don't have to reverse!

*

During my youth I was a committed member of Llangwrddon Young Farmers' Club. When I moved to live in Berthlwyd I joined the Llanilar club. A number of years later that one ceased to exist. But, we then realised that a new potential membership was to be found between Llangwrddon and Lledrod, as young people were kicking their heels with nowhere to go. The Llanilar club was re-formed and was lively and productive, lasting for some 11 years.

Olwen and I were privileged to be invited, along with others, to be club leaders. Members threw themselves into club activities, in particular those included in the YFC's yearbook. These included public speaking, which was of special interest to me. Others included farming activities such as fencing and stock judging.

But although we were a club of over 100 members by then, we were not overly proficient in the singing competitions. No-one, other than myself, was particularly interested in music. But we were brave enough to compete in the choir competition of the annual eisteddfod when it was held in Llandysul. We had a choir of 100 voices and I was the conductor. We sang the song 'Moliannwn' (Let's Rejoice) popularised by Bob Roberts, Tai'r Felin. We performed in unison, as the piece wasn't meant for four voices. Come the moment, we took to the stage and stood in order. I felt as if the weight of the whole world rested on my inadequate shoulders. Behind me sat the audience in the packed hall. In front of me were 100 young farmers. Before going through the motions of conducting, I tried to remind them of what was expected from them. And before raising my arms to prepare the accompanist I asked, 'Now then, any questions before we start?'

I was trembling like a leaf and, as I made to wave my arms, Richard Tudor raised his hand.

'Yes?' I asked. 'What do you want to know?'

'Just thinking, Dai,' he said innocently. 'Do we have to look at you?'

What a question! And what a time to ask it! We had been rehearsing for weeks! But that was the kind of relationship that existed between us as members. Despite everything we received a fulsome adjudication. We were placed third – out of three! But the important fact was that we had tried. It used to be the Olympic ideal, the taking part being more important that the winning. Not any more. Today, winning is the be all and end all – winning and crowing over it afterwards.

One great quality shared among all the members was that they had special parents who were all supportive of the club and anxious that we did well. In every competitive field they wanted us to be taught by the very best experts available. This was also true in my early days at Llangwrddon YFC.

We were taught the elements of public speaking by Hywel Thomas, Llanarth, whose mantra was: 'Always speak to a purpose. Avoid empty words. And think of your subject. Don't worry what anyone else has to say. Say what you have to say, and do so with dignity.'

Another who gave us his expertise was Heulyn Thomas. He was different. To begin with he was much larger physically, and had a deep, heavy voice. What with both Hywel and Heulyn, we would never be far from the best. We won the individual public speaking competition at county level more than once, and won a few times at national level too. Our public speaking team also won the Wales title.

It's strange how successes such as these can change the attitude of the whole neighbourhood. We didn't have any young people involving themselves in the community and other activities until the club was re-established. At least that's how it seemed. Then, as soon as the club reopened, they appeared. We would travel to the various events by bus. It would pick some of us up at the local pub. A tot or two at the Falcon Inn on Llanilar square would set us up nicely for the night. Then we would proceed, picking up other members on the way.

One notable achievement was winning the county

drama competition. We had made the top three on a few occasions. Two of our stalwarts in the drama section were Mari Vaughan Jones and Ann Vaughan. Mari had been interested in drama during her time in Cardiff and London. She was a popular member and we would often gather at her home for practices. She placed great emphasis on costume. Every item of apparel had to be perfect. I remember one year when we performed *The Practice*. At the dress rehearsal in Llanafan hall we tried out the costumes for the first time. The cast appeared one by one on stage as if in a mannequin parade. It was hilarious.

It is remarkable how many young people's careers have been nurtured by the YFC. The best example in Ceredigion is Ifan Gruffydd, or Ifan Tregaron, who is among Wales' most popular entertainers. Ifan is a product of the YFC through and through. Not only is he a top-class comedian and compère, he is also a playwright and drama adjudicator. He is true to the tradition of light entertainment greats such as Idwal Jones, Lampeter, who always maintained that comedy should be a serious business.

Ifan and I have worked and travelled together on many occasions. Nansi and John from Maestir-mawr were close friends that I had made through *Cefn Gwlad*. They grew vegetables – potatoes, carrots, swedes and cabbage – all kinds, which they sold at Swansea market. They would never miss the annual St David's Day concert held at Pontarddulais. One night, Ifan and I were on our way out of the hall there, ready to drive home, when our car was blocked by John's van. He poked his head through my car window.

'Here you are,' he said. 'Take these home with you.'

At his feet were two or three sacks full of vegetables. Ifan was laughing himself silly. Yes, Ifan and I are close friends. Whenever we meet at Tregaron mart and I succeed in making Ifan laugh, I feel as if I've achieved something special. We have travelled hundreds of miles together.

The highlight of the YFC year is the County Rally. Here in Ceredigion we have a custom that means that the winner of the Rally will, the following year, host the event. In our 11-year existence, Llanilar won the Rally five times. One of our most successful competitions was the Tableau. This involved creating a static scene based on a set theme. I remember when the Rally was held in Lledrod that our theme was Snow White and the Seven Dwarfs. For its centrepiece we built a small bungalow. When Ianto James, Henbant, saw it his response was, 'Well! Well! Dai, don't pull it down afterwards. This is by far the finest house in Lledrod!'

Before the Rally we would spend night after night searching for the various materials needed to build the Tableau set. Costumes would need to be found for the various characters as well. These were not easy tasks. One year we needed to build a Tableau based on a Welsh proverb. We decided on 'A fo ben, bid bont', meaning 'If you want to be a ruler, be a bridge'. We decided to build a bridge over a river, with one side reflecting poverty and the other wealth. We searched the neighbourhood for a thin-looking cockerel. We ultimately found one; it was almost as small as a sparrow. It had probably been on a Christmas diet. We then needed a fat gander for the other side. That was an easier task. The prime minister at the time was Margaret Thatcher. We chose one of the girls to portray her lying under the bridge. The idea was that crossing the bridge over Maggie would lead you to a better world.

I often emphasise my lack of formal education. The only training I ever received was what I learnt from my music tutors and through the Young Farmers' Club. In both cases I was taught how to feel comfortable among a crowd, and especially while facing an audience. And I, in turn, tried to convey that to club members. As a result, the members developed the same qualities. We went beyond the confines of the movement's curriculum. Among our extracurricular activities was an annual Thanksgiving service held at the chapel and the church alternatively. We organised musical evenings. We organised activities for the aged. We organised a carol service. We held a series of lectures. We organised exchange visits with other clubs.

One year, having won the county drama competition, we staged the winning one-act play with the two clubs that had been placed second and third. The event was held at Theatr y Werin, Aberystwyth. Our play had been written by the aforementioned J.R. Evans. This was an ambitious venture, as we were performing in a real theatre with all the latest props and lights. And I remember urging the cast, 'This is your chance to perform on a professional stage. Enjoy the experience. And as you perform in front of an appreciative audience, you can relish the fact that you will be creating something new.'

The theatre was packed. People tend to forget that the YFC Federation is a voluntary movement, with the members giving their time and effort freely – an amateur movement in the best sense of the word. Once, the movement was regarded as a lesser version of the Urdd (The Welsh League of Youth). But in recent years its activities have been given a national stage by S4C, something that has proved to be a great boost for everyone.

Of all the various YFC activities, I would claim that the most popular is the stock judging. There are many members, of course, who are not farmers, but every member has a connection with the farming community. Many ex-members of the Llanilar club, who cut their teeth judging stock at the Rally, went on to be judges themselves. Some have judged store sheep and cattle at the Royal Welsh Show and the Winter Fair. Many have also gone on to judge the craft and cooking sections. They began at club level but now they are teaching and advising others. Among those who have profited in such a way is my son John. Even though he does not like being in the public eye, he is very adept at judging lambs. He can pick and choose with the best. And all this is down to his experience as an ex-club member.

Looking back, we enjoyed a very successful 11 years. We provided a county chairman in John Llwynbrain. Others made it onto the county committee. Today, many ex-members are prominent in local activities, helping to keep local life and culture alive.

One change I would like to see is to do with the YFC age group specifications. At present the competing age ranges from 13 to 26. I would like to see this changed to 15 as the starting point, and terminating at 30. I feel that 13 is too early and 26 is certainly far too young an age to have to give up competing.

In many localities the YFC movement has indelibly stamped its mark on the neighbourhood. Young farmers today form the last bastion between rural people and the influx from towns and cities. They stand between us and oblivion, linguistically and culturally. The movement is much more than just a provider of entertainment for the farming community. It is the guardian of the Welsh language and everything connected with it too. It does so not by marching and carrying banners, but rather by living and speaking the language naturally day to day. It is a scandal that the Government, both in London and in Cardiff, does not provide more money for the movement.

The YFC's influence surpasses national boundaries. It has, for instance, campaigned for improving the supply and quality of clean water in the Sudan. I'm pleased to say that we in Llanilar contributed to this cause. We timed our campaign to begin on the Sunday morning prior to the Royal Welsh Show. It involved walking from Llanilar to Llanelwedd, a venture based on a Wellington-throwing relay. We went through a few pairs of Wellingtons before we reached journey's end! We left Llanilar, followed the Ystwyth valley up to New Row, and then across Cwmystwyth mountain. We didn't see many people initially but having reached Rhayader it became a different story. Some 30 of us scoured the town carrying buckets collecting money. We stopped cars; we begged, we pleaded. The response was fantastic. We ended the walk in the main stand of the Royal Welsh Show on the Sunday night.

At the Llanilar club we were lucky that our location was quite central, with the YFC headquarters only being an hour away. Llanilar is also only two hours from Cardiff in the south and Anglesey in the north.

As mentioned, people do tend to forget that there are always people supporting the members, their parents and families. I remember paying a tribute to one of our most loyal supporters, Mrs Davies, Brenar, at her funeral service. Her children, Sheila and Arwyn, were faithful members and Sheila had been County Queen. I remember coming out of Llanfihangel-y-Creuddyn church at Mrs Davies' funeral and seeing the cemetery – even the village itself – crowded with mourners who had come to pay their respects.

Things like that stick in the memory. It was a great privilege last year to be chosen as the Wales Young Farmers'

Clubs Federation national president for the third year in succession. In September 2016 I attended a dinner at Llannerchaeron marking the Wales YFC's 80th anniversary. There were some 300 present, and I was responsible for providing the meat. I bought a consignment of Rob Rattray's very best quality beef. Rob is always a great benefactor to good causes. At the 2010 Royal Welsh Show, sponsored by Ceredigion, he provided burgers which we sold with the profits going to the cause. Rob named them 'Mr President's Burgers' as I was the president that year. Ceredigion welcomed the Urdd National Eisteddfod at Llannerchaeron in 2010 also. Rob duly provided burgers for that good cause as well, naming them 'Mr Urdd's Burgers'.

When I was first appointed national president of the Wales YFC Federation, I succeeded Nigel Owens in the role. At the time he was over in South Africa refereeing an international rugby match. But he still went to the trouble of sending me a congratulatory telegram wishing me well on the night of my induction in Cardiff. It's worth noting that I was the first to introduce Nigel as a stand-up comedian when he appeared on stage in Conwy in a show televised by S4C.

The Llanilar Young Farmers' Club no longer exists. So many members had passed the competing age that we had no option but to close the club. But other local clubs are flourishing. The Lledrod club is just down the road. And who knows, the Llanilar club may be resurrected. I wouldn't be surprised. Young people come and go like the tide. It's ebb and flow. Let us hope that another high tide is on the way.

3

Swansong

No-one would be foolish enough to compare me with Frank Sinatra. But one Sunday night in Machynlleth I did feel a great affinity with Ol' Blue Eyes. Frank has become synonymous with the song 'My Way', a ballad that sums up his life. In it he faces his final curtain. And it was in a chapel in Machynlleth some three years ago that I announced my retirement from the stage as a solo artiste. I was acting as compère and my decision was sudden and decisive.

Since that night I have kept true to my decision. The Scriptures tell us that there is a time for everything. And that appearance in Machynlleth was the right time for me to end my singing career. It was time for my swansong. The word 'swansong' has an interesting origin. According to fable the swan, not noted for its purity of voice, sings its sweetest song as it dies. Not that I had any intention of dying. But I did feel that this was the moment to take the irrevocable decision. I had been considering it for a while but had kept putting it off.

Appearing on stage as well were past Blue Ribband winners at the National Eisteddfod. I myself was to join in in a few duets. And it was while I was listening to these stars that I made my decision. There is an old saying that implies that nothing is over until the fat lady sings. There was no fat lady on the bill that night. But she must have been there in spirit.

I still enjoy being on stage presenting or compering. But the singing is over. Singing is like playing rugby or soccer or being involved in athletics. If you want to compete at the highest level you must practice. And when I was singing I did practise a lot. I would practise the low scales while milking in the morning. Then, in the afternoon, I would practise the middle scales while driving the tractor. And in the evening I would practise the high scales while cleaning the milking shed. There the acoustics were perfect, what with the galvanised milk cans and the wall tiles. There was a good echo. It was what is known as acoustic resonance.

But in Machynlleth that night I came to the decision that this would be the end. I decided I would announce it from the stage. And I did. It meant there was no going back. No encore.

The main reason for making this decision in Machynlleth, rather than anywhere else, was that it was the perfect symbolic place to do so. The home of my very first tutor, Ifan Maldwyn Jones, was but a stone's throw away. He was one of three tutors who coached me, the other two being Redvers Llewellyn and Colin Jones. Without them I would have been a nonentity.

I should explain that Ifan's contribution was different to that of the other two. Both Redvers and Colin were voice coaches. Ifan's contribution had been interpretation, in particular interpreting the lyrics or librettos. Many of my songs were based on poetic works. So Ifan imbued in me the mindset of the poet, what he or she meant and how I should convey that meaning to the audience. He stressed that poetry should always be treated with respect.

The decision to bring my singing career to an end was difficult enough in itself. It meant ending what had been a way of life for years. But making that decision on the spur of the moment helped. I did not have to suffer the pangs of indecision. My one dread was having to refuse invitations to sing from old friends. And I realised that, should I accede to one, then others would be disappointed. But it was full stop. Or you could say that the fool stopped.

Some singers' voices develop late. Mine matured at an early age. I won the National Eisteddfod Blue Ribband when I was only 25. The family has a singing tradition. My grandfather was a fine tenor and was coached by Walford Davies. My father was a good baritone. But my decision to take to the stage was because I felt it was a means of communicating with people: an interrelation between myself and the public. I love people. I love being with people. Appearing in front of an audience of 60,000 people wouldn't bother me one bit. However, compare this with running my dogs in sheepdog trials – another of my delights. Should there be only two or three people standing behind me as I put my dogs through their paces, my legs would turn to jelly.

I might as well confess, I am not a musician. A singer, yes. But there is a difference. For one thing I can't read music. Fortunately I have a good ear. Having heard a song once, I will not forget it. It will be ingrained on my memory as indelibly as the Lord's Prayer. I would buy recordings, play them over and over again, and memorise them note for note, word for word.

I mentioned in my previous autobiography the invitation I received to study music in Italy. A few days after my success at the Llangollen International Eisteddfod in 1970, I was out ploughing grassland. There I was, perched on my blue tractor with no cab, being bombarded by seagulls using me as target practice, when three strangers approached me. I stopped work and took them to the house for a cup of tea. I refused their kind invitation to go to Italy. I didn't have to think twice. I was a farmer. I am a farmer. I will always be a farmer first and foremost. I will never leave the countryside permanently as long as I have breath left in my body.

I was, on the other hand, interested in opera. I joined the Aberystwyth Operatic Society. I well remember playing the part of Filch in *The Beggar's Opera*. At the dress rehearsal, in my ragged costume and plastered in make-up as dark as gravy browning, I decided to take a break to go home and do the milking. It was a Sunday evening and, as I reached Llanilar, the faithful were on their way to church and chapel. I heard later that many of them had wondered who was that strange man who had been driving Dai Jones' car. When I went to call the cows they stampeded! Even my dogs ran away. They must have believed that there was a mobile scarecrow at large.

Of course, as someone who was in the public eye, I was asked to perform duties other than singing. One request was to pay a tribute at funerals, especially tributes to those I had often competed against at sheepdog trials. The first was for Meirion Jones, Pwllglas, Ruthin, the sage of the trials circuit. Meirion was a man of the people. His son still lives in Pencoed in the county. Following my tribute I was myself complimented for my oration by another of the greats of the sheepdog trials. Idris Morgan, Bancllyn, on Mynydd Bach, went as far as to compare me with a giant of the pulpit, Philip Jones, Porthcawl. Now that was a compliment!

Here again, when paying a public tribute, my words come not from a prepared speech but from the heart. And you can't eulogise someone you haven't known well. As we all grow older, unfortunately, such events occur far too often these days. And requests to take part on such occasions are impossible to refuse.

The most difficult occasion was when I was invited to address the mourners at the funeral of the young daughter of a neighbour. Gwenno Tudor was buried on the day she would have celebrated her 19th birthday. Carmel chapel in Llanilar overflowed. It was a distressful experience. I felt as if there was a barrier between me and the Almighty. But such an experience brings with it some peace of mind to those who grieve. Some sort of closure or release. When I am asked to perform such a task I do consider it a privilege.

There is a fable that relates a Persian king issuing a challenge to his wise men. He charges them to create a phrase that would be appropriate for any occasion. The phrase chosen was, 'And this shall pass.' The fable warns us that all good things come to an end. It also encourages us, saying that all grieving will eventually end as well.

I am forever grateful that I have been given some sort of talent for performing in public. It brings me a personal satisfaction. All the better if it also brings fulfilment to others. And it pleases me that what little talent I have was nurtured on eisteddfod stages or at agricultural showgrounds. And, that it was obtained through my own endeavours without any favours or family connections or influences.

My first successes came on the Young Farmers' Club stage. I then graduated to small village eisteddfods. It was at the Ty'n-y-graig eisteddfod that I won my first trophy. Ty'n-y-graig is a small hamlet on the road between Pontrhydfendigaid and Aberystwyth. It has less than a dozen houses and a chapel. You could easily drive through it without noticing it. And it was there at Caradog chapel that I won my first cup. This was typical of the kind of small eisteddfod where I cut my teeth competitively. They would be held in chapels, vestries and small halls. In chapels the stage would be the deacons' pew. In such places I would be one of around a dozen competing for the champion solo, well after midnight, and facing an audience of a few dozen.

At the time I would never have dreamt that later in life I would face an audience of thousands at Madison Square Garden in Manhattan in New York City as a guest singer of the Rhos Male Voice Choir. Madison Square Garden is among the most fabled venues in the world. It hosts all kinds of events, from concerts to sporting occasions. Elvis appeared there. John Lennon sang there. Joe Louis fought there. And I still can hardly believe that I, an insignificant farmer from Llanilar, also appeared there.

I also appeared in New York with the Pendyrus Male Voice Choir to a packed house at the Metropolitan Pavilion. During the interval members of the audience, mostly descendants of Welsh immigrants, joined us for a chat over a cup of tea. They couldn't believe that they could enjoy such a musical feast for an entrance fee of just one dollar. For the second half, Pendyrus' legendary flamboyant conductor, Glynne Jones, summoned all of us, choir members and guests, onstage. He addressed the audience with a great speech and led us in singing the American and the Welsh national anthems.

It was a bizarre experience, for someone raised among the Cardiganshire hills, to try to sleep to the sounds of police sirens and awake to the sounds of traffic rather than the crowing of cockerels. When you find yourself standing before a mirror in a luxury hotel bedroom dressed like a turkey for a poultry show, you have to wonder whether you are dreaming.

Memorable as such occasions are, I still can't forget those early years in such places as Caradog chapel, sipping tea in the lobby and awaiting my turn to compete in the deacons' pew. Even as I stood in the splendour of Madison Square Garden I was, in spirit, back at Caradog chapel in Ty'n-y-graig.

On a slightly more localised level than the eisteddfods were the smaller competitive meetings, the 'Cwrdd Bach'. I remember competing at Tabor chapel in Llangwrddon. The adjudicators were John Jones Bryngalem and Mair Meiarth. They invited me to their own 'Cwrdd Bach' in Bwlchllan. After the competition I went to Mair's home for a cup of tea. She kept the local shop. I have attended lavish garden parties at Buckingham Palace but nothing could compare with the spread and the welcome offered by Mair.

Singers today can earn good money. Back then we competed for a few shillings, a medal, or, if lucky, a cup. Such prizes, though, couldn't compare with the words of praise proffered by a generous adjudicator. We, the competitors, appreciated and treasured any advice, even criticism. Praise would be the ultimate prize.

Following the eisteddfod circuit was fun. Something memorable would happen in every eisteddfod, something that would be talked about for weeks. There would always be a repartee between certain members of the audience and the compère, the adjudicators or the competitors. What happened at Lledrod eisteddfod back in the 1960s was typical. There was a well-known trader, known as Bowker, who would buy or sell anything in the area. On stage in Lledrod, Rhiannon Caffrey was reciting a well-known piece about selling slaves. In the poem there was an analogy to the various religious denominations. The poem went something like this:

What about the Methodists?
Will they buy the slaves? No!
Will the Baptists buy them? No!
Will the Independents buy them? No!

Then came a shout from the back. 'Why don't you try Bowker? He'll buy them!'

Then there were the Christmas meetings. I remember being invited to sing at what was called the 'Christmas Tree' in Trisant. There were some five or six of us, including Billy and Edwina Morris, Llanilar; Carol from Pontrhydygroes; Alun Jenkins, Capel Bangor, and myself. We were not being paid, naturally. I overheard a discussion between members of the organising committee.

'We should give them something.'

'But they've said they don't want anything.'

'We can't let them go home empty-handed. It wouldn't be nice.'

Then, following more discussions, over came Jim Powell.

'Thanks a lot,' he said. 'We very much appreciate your

contribution. We've decided to give you something for your trouble. Here's ten shillings. Share it out between you.'

The money wasn't important. We would continue to follow the circuit, very much a local one in those days. Trisant, Pontrhydygroes and Ysbyty Ystwyth were all within a few miles of each other. Today, both Trisant and Ysbyty Ystwyth chapels are dwellings, while Pontrhydygroes chapel has long since been turned into flats. Yet the legacy continues. A new generation carries on the singing tradition. A prime example is soprano Rhian Lois, who is of world class. Then there are the Evans brothers of Trisant. One of them, Robin Lyn, is a Blue Ribband winner both in the under 25 and open sections.

Such singers have risen from the hinterlands of Wales. They have inherited the tradition. Not so long ago such neighbourhoods could boast three or four choirs. The Pontrhydygroes area is a typical example. Jim Powell ran his own choir for years. Delyth Hopkin Evans, Lois' mother, has been organising and conducting choirs for quite some time too. And although the eisteddfods are gone, as I said, the legacy continues.

As a farmer I would spend my working days on the land among the animals. The usual pleasures included the mart and an occasional sheepdog trial, an agricultural show or a farm sale. The singing offered a totally different escape from daily tasks. As well as singing as a soloist in an eisteddfod or a concert, I would also be invited to appear with various male voice choirs. Nothing pleased me more than being

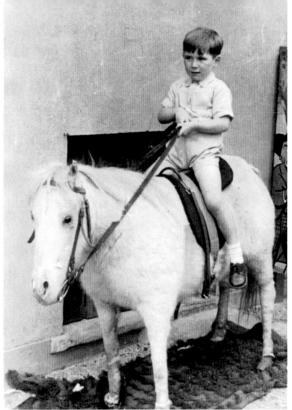

The little pony which carried me as a child.

The reluctant musician playing the fiddle at Llangwrddon school.

On the right, with Glenys, my sister, and my brother, Trefor, on the left.

Olwen, the young farmer – a photograph taken after she won the Duke of Edinburgh Award.

Four generations – John and me, with my mother and Celine.

Our son, John, with Ella on the tractor.

Ella, with one of her favourite animals, Rob the sheepdog.

The two sisters, Celine and Ella.

Ella (back) with her brother and sister, Aaron and Leila.

Those of us who go on holiday together annually – Carys, Gwen, Ifan, Mari, Charles, Huw, me and Olwen, in a boat on the Norfolk Broads.

Smart young thing trying to catch Olwen's attention.

Just look at my pose!

Jen and me in the *Siôn a Siân* days.

Standing between Janice Ball and Rosalind on the *Siôn a Siân* set. During my time on the series Janice accompanied me on the piano for 700 songs.

New Year's Eve television programme with Hywel Gwynfryn. Highly appropriately, I sang 'Donald, Where's Your Troosers?' with Jimmy Shand's band.

Eric Jones and me at the top of Bwlch y Moch, my first experience of abseiling.

On the piste with Wil Hafod, or Herr Wil as he is known by the locals.

The whole crew who filmed *Ar y Piste* (On the Piste).

Grape picking with Now from the singing group Hogia Llandegái.

Filming *Cefn Gwlad* with my wonderful friend, Trebor Gwanas.

Joni Moch was the subject of one of the most popular *Cefn Gwlad* programmes.

William Cae'r Berllan giving me instruction, along with a stable lad, on how to train a shire horse.

With Wil Llannor at the Ballinasloe horse fair in County Gallway, Ireland.

Sitting scared witless in a coracle.

With Wyn Gruffydd, one of my co-presenters at the Royal Welsh Show.

Enjoying a moment's peace in the majesty of the mountains.

The filming crew on one of the early series of *Cefn Gwlad*.

Film crew enjoying its visit to Dingle in the west of Ireland.

This programme followed the life of Enduro champion, David Jones from Llanidloes.

Don Garreg Ddu enrapt watching the wrestling.

With Ernest Naish filming *Away with Dai*. Ernest Naish was the father of double bass soloist Bronwen Naish.

The dear, departed Richard Tŷ'n Bryn, near Llanegryn.

With Wil Llys, Penisa'r Waun's team-horses.

With Rhisiart ap Rhys Owen from Llanymynech, one of Europe's most prominent veterinary surgeons.

Riding with Daff, the shepherd, on Mynydd Du.

Filming amongst the splendour of Hafod y Llan.

My dear companion, Don Garreg Ddu, with his mare, Bess.

An opportunity to discuss the day's work with John, our son.

invited to sing with some of the south Wales valleys choirs. I would share the stage with many lads who spent their days underground. Then, by late evening, they would be singing like songbirds released from their cages.

They lived in a world totally alien to me. I remember the first time I went down to the valleys, an innocent Cardi. In the bar they sank pints like thirsty bullocks. To them I wasn't Dai – I was Defi. In the north I was Dafydd. In Ceredigion I was, and always will be, Dai. Singing with the valley lads and socialising with them afterwards was both a pleasure and a privilege.

The choir members of north-east Wales were just the same, and also from a coal mining background mostly. I also remember singing with the Rhos Male Voice Choir at the Philharmonic Hall in Liverpool. The musical director was Sir Charles Groves. And there was I, a yokel from Llangwrddon, sharing the platform with a musical giant. Yes, I shared the stage with some of the greats. There was none greater than Richard Rees, Pennal. Add to the list Elwyn Jones, Llanbedrog; Tom and Trebor Gwanas; Tom Bryniog; Ifan and Ifor Lloyd; Berwyn Davies, Felinfach; and Washington James, Cenarth. Then sopranos and contraltos such as Margaret Lewis Jones, Margaret Williams, Jean Evans, Pontarddulais, and Glenys Dowdle. Their names resonate and echo past pleasures.

Many of these were farmers themselves, of course. I consider farming to be a privileged vocation. It is a mission. You strive to improve the standard of your stock.

You strive to improve the quality of your pasture. You strive to improve the boundaries of your land. You strive to improve your own standard of living. You strive to maintain the succession. The continuation of the family farm is a priority.

A great emphasis is placed on the environment these days. Our forefathers always cared for the upkeep and beauty of the countryside over the centuries without any compulsion or remuneration. But, today, farmers are plagued by people carrying briefcases who look around and jot down details in notebooks. And, of course, there is the ever-present laptop or tablet. Why? Is there any need for such bureaucracy? Successful soccer or rugby teams are not dependent on civil servants. And how can you run an industry ruled by people who have no knowledge of the business world? In the olden days, before you could follow the plough, you first had to learn to lead a horse.

But back to the performing! It certainly opened doors for me – and performing is a joy in itself. It has taken me to different parts of the world. And one thing I've noticed when performing abroad is that audiences appreciate hearing me sing the songs of my own country. Of course I also include a song or two from the country I happen to be visiting. We Welsh, unlike the English, are fortunate in this respect. As we ourselves speak and write a phonetic language, it makes it easier for us to pronounce the words of Italian and Spanish songs. I must admit that I have found French to be difficult. My limit is 'Plaisir d'Amour'.

One of my greatest pleasures is presenting my Sunday night radio programme, *Ar Eich Cais*. I get to read requests for songs from listeners from all over Wales and beyond. Often I am overcome by some of the sentiments expressed. Reading listeners' letters and replying on air is like an intimate conversation. Nothing pleases me more than hearing comments at Welshpool mart the following Monday from some of those who had listened the previous night.

'Well, Dai, so-and-so was great singing on your programme last night. And what you said! Really interesting.'

Realising that my comments have led to a discussion pleases me. Indeed, it gives me a thrill. And those letters I receive in response to my remarks are priceless too. I recently received a letter from an elderly man who had lost his wife. He felt lonely, he said, especially as it was Palm Sunday. He requested a record that would bring him comfort. Responding to such a request creates a kind of rapport. I feel that I am not only pleasing the person who sends the request but also enriching my own life.

Then there are the requests from children. A young girl, perhaps, wants a record played for her aunt on a special birthday. I often ask myself, what I have done to deserve being able to perform such a service? It is a privilege, one that I am eternally grateful for. I feel that I am filling a void in people's lives, some who may live all alone and feel lonely. Sometimes, I am personally asked to choose an appropriate record to suit them. This then brings pleasure to me, as well as to those making the request, and I often choose artistes I may have shared a stage with.

It is sad that the BBC no longer has numerous tapes of old classics. For example, there is a dearth of mixed choir performances on record, but many choral classics have disappeared, including recordings by famous choirs such as the Rhos Male Voice Choir. It never ceases to amaze me that many of our great Welsh choirs come from deprived areas, such as the coalfields. Singing, to them, was an escape from their hardship, and as natural as keeping racing pigeons and greyhounds or watching rugby. Then, with the closure of the pits, the industry that bound the communities together disappeared. With it died the culture that was synonymous with that industry. In one respect, of course, bringing an end to men having to crawl like moles underground for their crust was a blessing. But something important was lost forever. A way of life disappeared. Forms of enjoyment disappeared. Community life was lost.

Whatever, I brought my singing career to an end. An activity that had been such a part of my life for years was no longer. Indeed, it was far more than an activity. It was pure pleasure. And as I look back I can say, like Sinatra, that I have lived a life that's full. I have also travelled each and every highway. Whether the road I travelled was straight or winding is another matter.

4

Honours

OVER THE YEARS I have been honoured many times and in many ways. Most honours have arrived in the past few years. I mention these honours, not to brag but as a way of thanking those who bestowed them. I have to pinch myself to believe that an ordinary farm lad from Cardiganshire could receive such awards.

Let us go back decades to begin with, back to the Llangollen International Musical Eisteddfod Blue Ribband in 1970. Just a month later I won the Blue Ribband at the National Eisteddfod in Ammanford. Those were the highlights of my singing career. As I have mentioned, eisteddfods, big and small, opened doors for me.

Nothing compares to the eisteddfod stage for creating a rapport with your audience. No-one is more shrewd than an eisteddfod audience. There was a time when heckling from some members of the audience was something to expect, especially after stop-tap. For example, the Bont boys were famous for their heckling. The heckler-in-chief was their chauffeur Dic Davies, or Dic Bach as he was always referred to. Dic turned heckling into an art. Yet, should you win the

Bont boys' favour, you would evidently be a success. And I was accepted by them early on.

The eisteddfod was a good place too for me to get to know myself as a competitor. In local parlance, it was the ideal place for you 'to get to know your size'. After all, if you don't get to know yourself, you will not be able to assess other people. It is said that whoever gets to know others is wise, but whoever is able to know oneself is enlightened.

Then there was the other great influence, the Royal Welsh Show. I have been commentating there now for more years than I care to remember. This opportunity came about with the retirement of the late Llew Phillips. Welsh commentary was all-important to Llew. He ensured that it was pure, yet easily understandable, Welsh; the kind of language that ordinary people could appreciate. He strongly believed that the language deserved centre stage and should not be pushed to the periphery. He was determined that Welsh should be heard in the main ring. Later, my old friend Charles Arch was appointed Welsh announcer and commentator at the show. Charles and I worked together for many happy years, thoroughly enjoying every minute.

As part of the TV offering these days, we present an hour-long programme on S4C as a prelude to the show. Then, during the show itself, I share the commentating with presenters such as Wyn Gruffydd and Tweli Griffiths, and it is still a pure joy to do so.

The greatest change over the years has been the increased amount of live broadcasting from the Royal Welsh Show, and I have been privileged to be a part of these programmes. It is difficult to comprehend the fact that the eyes of the world are potentially fixed on us throughout the show now. I can walk along Princes Street in Edinburgh or Grafton Street in Dublin and be recognised and greeted by name. That brings me no little pleasure. Television has made the world smaller for us by bringing people closer together. Like that famous beer, S4C reaches parts that other television channels cannot reach.

I have received all kinds of honours in recognition of my work with the Royal Welsh Show. I received the Sir Bryner Jones Award for my services to the show, something that, to me, is synonymous with winning the Blue Ribband for singing. The award is presented annually to someone who has made a special contribution to agriculture, which can vary from erecting specialised buildings to growing pasture or breeding stock. The Sir Bryner Jones Award therefore shares a shelf in my glass cabinet with my two Blue Ribbands won at the National and at the International Eisteddfod.

I was awarded the MBE, again as a recognition of my contribution to farming. I would like to believe that my work with the Royal Welsh Show had something to do with it. As already noted, in 2010 Ceredigion was the host county. Although the show is held perpetually in Llanelwedd, designated counties host the event in turn and are obliged to finance it. Today there is great emphasis on branding, and the 2010 show was named 'Sioe'r Cardis' or 'The Cardis'

Show'. The designated county is given two years to prepare and to raise the necessary funds. The same principle applies to the National Eisteddfod, except that districts host the Eisteddfod rather than counties. The National Eisteddfod is also peripatetic, alternating between north and south Wales every year.

For the 2010 Cardis' Show I was made president. This was one of the greatest honours I could ever receive. Indeed, as far as agriculture is concerned, this rates as the highest. I organised a hard-working team who involved themselves in all kinds of activities county-wide. Many of these ventures were auctions where I often acted as auctioneer. The response was overwhelming. I remember selling a bottle of whisky for £500 and a shepherd's crook for the same amount. All these events, as well as boosting funds, also publicised the main goal of raising a target fund of some £200,000, the kind of sum raised by other counties in the past. Some of our events brought in between £10,000 and £12,000 each. We designed fashionable items of clothing bearing the logo 'Sioe'r Cardis 2010'. This venture in itself brought in £47,000. In all, we raised the amazing total of £450,000. Who dares to accuse the Cardi of being tight-fisted?

Money, of course, wasn't everything. The greatest offering anyone can give to the Royal Welsh is a practical contribution. And the Royal Welsh is our social home. No other four-day agricultural show in the world attracts more people through its turnstiles. Yet the thousands who throng there make up one big family. And through it all, both languages walk side by side.

*

I came up with the idea of producing a TV documentary on each year's host county, to be televised just before the Royal Welsh started. The proposal was accepted by S4C and it gave us the opportunity to portray that particular county, its attributes and peculiarities, its modes of farming and some of its characters.

To coincide with the Cardis' Show, among the prominent exhibitors interviewed and filmed was the Wilson family of Tregibby near Cardigan. The fourth generation of the Wilsons now breed and exhibit Holsteins, and more recently Jerseys. They can be proud of the fact that, back in 2010, a prominent judge pronounced that the family owned the best Holstein cow in the world. By then, Dalesend Storm Maude, a remarkable 12-year-old cow, had won the Royal Welsh Championship four times and the British Championship five times, a record. She had produced 124 tons of milk and had given birth to eight calves. She belonged to the fourth generation of her lineage, and three generations were still milking. Indeed, so famous was Maude that a ceramic company produced a limited edition china figurine of her.

We also visited Troedyraur Farm in Brongest, home of two of the most faithful supporters of the Royal Welsh, the late Tom and Lilian Evans. Both had been show presidents, with their tradition of pig breeding continuing via their son Teifi, and his own son Rhys. Troedyraur Farm has championed the Welsh pig over the years; it is a fairly rare breed that is gradually growing in popularity now. Both Teifi and his son intend to bring in new blood by experimenting with different breeds. Teifi is a great believer in finding pigs with a certain progeny, provided the animals are not too closely related. And it was so good to film at Troedyraur and see the lineage of the Evans family itself continuing, with Teifi and Rhys carrying on Tom and Lilian's pioneering work.

I then travelled to the north of the county to Cerrig Caranau, known locally as Cerrig Trane, between Borth and Tre Taliesin. There, Geraint and Eifion Jenkins, like their father, grandfather and great-grandfather before them, keep Welsh Black cattle. This breed is important to the Jenkinses not only because of its native roots but also because of its substantial milk output. Welsh Black cows still produce a heavy yield even after they turn ten years old. They are also hardy cattle that can remain outside well into the winter season. Both Geraint and Eifion are enthusiastic members of Talybont YFC.

We filmed one of our most successful money-raising events, the picture auction. Central to it was an original painting by Aneurin Jones of Cardigan depicting scenes from the first ever Royal Welsh Show. Prints of the picture in a limited edition were also for sale. The original sold for £15,000 and was handed back to the show authorities.

It hangs in the International Pavilion on the showground. The person behind the idea of commissioning the painting was Roland Williams, founder of Greenlands Insurance Services in Aberystwyth. Roland has been a keen breeder of Suffolk sheep since the 1980s, and on the programme I interviewed him and his children, Buddug and Ilan. Roland decided to keep the Suffolk because of their particular shape and style. He also breeds Texel and Southdown on land belonging to the National Library. The flock's prefix is Greenlands.

We couldn't ignore the horses, naturally. We went to the Frongoy Stud, Pennant, a placed steeped in the Welsh cob tradition. There the Jones family have bred cobs for generations. The three brothers, Isaac, David John and Brynmor, were legends of the cob world. Brynmor was still with us in 2010. He was 93 years old and was sorry to have to give the show a miss that year. He comforted himself in knowing that he could watch S4C's extensive television coverage.

Dafydd, their father, was himself a great character. Breeders from south Wales would often call at Frongoy, and Dafydd would describe his sons' various attributes to them. Brynmor, according to him, was the machinery specialist. David John was the horse man and Isaac, again according to the father, was the expert on women! The old man's perceptive summing up of his sons' characteristics is still part of local folklore.

Their direct descendant, Gwyn, had been invited to judge

at the Royal Welsh in 2010. And it was from Gwyn that I received the best advice ever for any prospective judge.

'First, choose the horse you would most like to take home with you. Place this horse as your standard and go on from there.'

The family tradition continues with Gwyn's sons, Dafydd and Siôn. They, however, breed sheep, including Kerry Hill and Suffolk.

Next it was to Fronfedw, Ciliau Aeron, to film Dan Davies and his son Rhidian's herd of Blonde d'Aquitaine. They came upon the breed by chance. Back in 1985 Dan went to Sennybridge to buy a bull. He had never cast eyes on this particular breed before. But he took a chance and ended up happy. This French breed is notable for the quality of its meat. And Dan learnt the lesson that the best meat on the Blonde d'Aquitaine is found where the beast can feel the sun.

Another venture in 2010 was the publication of a bilingual book, *Ymlaen â'r Sioe / On With the Show*, researched and written by Charles Arch and Lyn Ebenezer. We filmed the authors at the Great Abbey Farm in Strata Florida where Charles was born and raised. This wasn't the only volume to be published for the occasion that year either. Dr Wynne Davies of the Ceulan Stud also published his book *Welsh Ponies and Cobs: Ceredigion Champions*.

Numerous open days were arranged up and down the county. In Aberystwyth we organised a parade of farm animals, an event that brought the country to town. In attendance was Teleri Jenkins-Davies, the show's Lady Ambassador. We felt that the ladies had not been given enough prominence previously. This time we gave them leading roles. The TV programme also featured Margaret Gerrard, one of the arts and crafts section judges at the show. I visited her at her home in Llangoedmor and was shown her various creations. Margaret specialised in handicraft, especially pillows and traditional Welsh blankets, knitting and crotchet work.

In Aberaeron I did something that I had never done before and will never do again. In front of the cameras I modelled at a fashion show. I even went as far as to wear a pair of jeans. Again, this is something that I will never repeat, especially having encountered the problem of pulling them up over my ample stomach. But even worse than wearing jeans was the fact that I had to wear shorts! My legs hadn't been seen in public for quite some time!

At three different locations we held open days for the Welsh cobs, visiting Dai and Siân Harris at the Pennal Stud, Blaenpennal; Huw and Carys Davies at Drefaes Stud near Llandysul, and Peter and Ann Jones at the Menai Stud in Prengwyn. Pennal Brynmor, from the Pennal Stud, had won the George Prince of Wales Cup at the Royal Welsh the previous year.

It is customary for the funds raised by the host county to go towards a project earmarked by the show authorities. The money raised for the Cardis' Show was designated to be spent on the uncompleted food pavilion. This was agreed with the understanding that there would be an opportunity to influence the other counties to contribute towards a building for the horse section at some time in the future. This was appropriate considering the unique relationship between Ceredigion and the cob. The Welsh cob and pony are a worldwide attraction, and it would only be right that there were a suitable building for them on the showground.

Yes, it was a very special year, and being privileged to be president of the show was one of the highlights of my life. During the show, Olwen and I were fêted like a king and queen!

*

In a totally different sphere I was made president of the Colin Jones Singers. The 'Maestro', as he is known, has now retired. This is a man who toiled at the coalface as a young man. He won a scholarship allowing him to study at a school of music and was later appointed as a voice lecturer in Manchester. He then, of course, became synonymous with the Rhos Male Voice Choir and formed the Colin Jones Singers, a group of talented singers forming a 100-strong choir that toured the world. Many of the choir's members were seasoned eisteddfod singers, such as Tom Bryniog and Trebor Gwanas and his two sons. Acting as president of that choir was a privilege. I visited France with them and the French loved their singing.

Another great honour was being made a Fellow of Aberystwyth University and an Honorary Masters of Arts by the University of Wales. And consider this: although I only received what was then referred to as a secondary modern school education – with more marks on my hands from a cane than from ink – am I now allowed to use the prefix 'Doctor' in front of my name? Maybe not...

Another great honour was winning the top prize at the Smithfield Show with my Welsh Black bullock. This was the very first time a Welsh Black bullock had won the Queen Mother's Cup. Although it was a bullock which I had bought, I perfected and prepared it for showing. I had bought it especially for a *Cefn Gwlad* programme so that I could show viewers all the work needed to nurture and prepare such an animal. Winning the award was a bonus, especially winning it at Smithfield, the world's most prestigious event for showing store cattle.

A year later I won the competition for the best home-grown bullock at the Royal Welsh, a creature that I myself had bred. To crown it all, I was invited to be president of the Welsh Black Society in its centenary year. Add to all that also the vice-presidency of the Welsh Pony & Cob Society, the presidency of the Wales branch of the International Sheep Dog Trials, and representing Wales in the international trials competition.

Last year the International Sheep Dog Trials were held in Tywyn in north Wales and I went there with Charles Arch and Huw Aberffrydlan, Llanwrin. Appropriately, the president was another old and close friend of mine, Eirian Morgan. I can't remember a better international trialing event. Apart from the success of the event, you couldn't find a superior setting. It was held in the shadow of Craig y Deryn and Cader Idris. And to cap it all, the overall winner was a Welshman, Kevin Evans from Libanus, Powys. Wales won the prize for the team event and, among the 15 dogs in the last event, seven were Welsh sheepdogs. And the driving event was also won by Welshman, Aled Owen of Tynant, Corwen.

To turn to the media world and complete the picture, I was made a Fellow of BAFTA Wales. I'm not one who is overly fond of ceremony. I am not a celeb, thank God. But receiving the BAFTA crowned my work in the media.

Should I have to choose the ultimate honour though, it would have to be the fact that the viewers, when asked to vote for their favourite television programme in 2002 – the year that marked S4C's twentieth anniversary – plumped for *Cefn Gwlad*. To me, nothing can beat that. But I would be the first to admit that this wasn't a personal honour. No, it reflected the success of the whole production team.

5

Coming and going

TRAVELLING THE WORLD has meant I've done my fair share of flying. Yet, for one who is frightened of cats, I have never been afraid of flying. Flying cats, maybe. And sailing? No, I don't fancy that one bit either. In fact, I try to keep well away from any activity that has anything to do with water. I have been offered the chance to provide entertainment on various cruise ships. I have turned them all down. I couldn't imagine waking up in bed at night knowing that there wasn't a field or a hedge within miles and that there were fathoms of water beneath me.

No, give me a plane any time. Although I wouldn't fancy long-haul flights these days. I wouldn't, for instance, fancy flying once again halfway across the world to somewhere like New Zealand. That great character Eirwyn Pontsiân had a saying: 'It's worth leaving so that you can come back. If you don't leave, you won't come back.'

Lisi Pengelli would say something similar. I would often stop to gossip with Lisi. After a while I would tell her: 'I'd better go Lisi, so that I can come back.'

And Lisi would reply, 'Yes, you had better go or you'll never come back.'

That sentiment could well be applied to me. During the 20 years since I published my first autobiography I have visited many foreign lands. And, true to Eirwyn Pontsiân and Lisi Pengelli's advice, I have always returned.

One television documentary took me to America to film a millionaire whose roots were in Cardiganshire. Businessman Bob Evans' father had emigrated from the hills of Bwlchllan and Penuwch to Ohio. He followed his forebears, the Edwards family of Brynele, Bwlchllan, who joined other relatives and neighbours in an exodus from the area to Ohio in the 1830s. The Edwards' were and are a notable family. BBC newsreader Huw Edwards is a direct descendant, as is Dafydd Edwards, the tenor from Bethania.

The man I went to see was Bob Evans, and he founded a chain of restaurants on the same pattern as the Little Chefs we have over here. Bob, a larger-than-life character, was known as the Sausage Millionaire. When we first met he addressed me in his broad American drawl: 'I see you ain't got a hat, Dai!'

I told him that I did own one but that I'd left it at home. But he insisted that I should have one. He believed that a man without a hat was naked. 'You've gotta have a real American hat,' he urged.

And he handed me one, a good one at that. It was a Stetson, big enough for me to dip sheep in. The Stetson was first designed to be worn by gold prospectors in Colorado. Later, cowboys claimed it as their own. It is also known as the ten-gallon hat. It went well with my ten-gallon stomach! It was also a ten-day hat as I wore it for all ten days I was out there.

As his nickname implied, Bob had made his fortune from producing sausages, later to become the staple fare at his restaurant chain. He was a hugely popular man. Every time he turned up at one of his outlets he would be surrounded immediately by his customers.

On my first morning he asked me what I'd like for breakfast. I told him that I'd like a typical traditional American breakfast. As everyone knows, I am a noted big eater. But when my breakfast arrived, even I was flabbergasted. The plate was heaped with half a dozen pancakes dripping with maple syrup. And that was just the beginning.

'You ain't seen nothin' yet!' drawled Bob.

He then plonked in front of me a 12-ounce steak. It could have doubled as a doorstop. To follow there was black coffee, gallons of it. Bob had brought me the sort of breakfast he imagined I'd like.

'I can see what kind of a guy you are,' he said.

Yes, Bob was a perceptive man. Having stuffed my stomach it was time for me to look around. Bob's grandson was there too to accompany me. He drove a car that was almost as large as Llanilar's village hall. He drove me along a road named after his grandfather, The Bob Evans Highway, a section of Route 35. I've visited the United States a good half-dozen times but it was Bob who showed me the real America.

His wife Jewell was a lovely lady. Upon meeting her I could have mistaken her for a Welsh country girl. Her welcome was a Welsh welcome. The first thing she did was ask me if I fancied a cup of tea. The family home was also Welsh in its décor, from the pictures on the wall to the furniture. Jewell had met some of the most important people in the USA but she welcomed me as if I was the most important person in the world.

Bob was born in Wood County, Ohio, where his father and uncle farmed rented land. The family then moved to Gallia County where other family members had already settled. The name 'Gallia' reflects the influence of the early French settlers. But so many Welsh immigrants from Cardiganshire then flocked there that it was referred to as 'Little Cardiganshire'.

Bob's father opened a grocery store, while the son did well educationally by graduating in veterinary medicine. Upon marrying Jewell Waters in 1940, they bought a restaurant in Gallipolis but Bob sold it to a friend when he joined the army. After finishing his military service he bought a farm and, as part of the venture, he established a 12-stool diner. He then began producing sausages made from meat from his own pigs. This marked the beginning of a venture named Bob Evans Farms. That first small restaurant is still flourishing and now seats 134 diners.

The business expanded rapidly and by 1957 Bob owned four sausage factories. Unfortunately, other local restaurants were reluctant to buy Bob's product. Bob's response was to establish his own chain of eateries. Today there are 600 restaurants in 24 states. In January 2017 Bob Evans Restaurants business was sold to a private equity company for $565 million.

Bob had retired as director and president of the company in 1986, and died in 2007 aged 89. He championed local country life until the end. He is the only person in history to have been honoured three times by the US National Wildlife Federation. He was a staunch supporter of the young farmers' organisation, a movement that corresponds to our federation of Young Farmers' Clubs.

Bob and Jewell and their six children lived near Rio Grande in Ohio, an area settled by dozens of Cardis in the 1830s. The family farmhouse is now registered as a place of historical interest. It houses a museum that exhibits antiques and country crafts. Each October the Bob Evans Farm Festival is held. By the way, I was not allowed to keep the Stetson. A Cardi is always a Cardi and, as a true Cardi, Bob wanted his hat back!

I remember John Nantllwyd, having seen the Ohio TV documentary, describing it to a fellow worshipper at Soar y Mynydd chapel: 'You'll never believe this,' said John, 'but this chap from Bwlchllan was making sausages. He has this big contraption. He pushes a whole pig in one end and sausages pour out of the other end.'

His friend asked, 'What if he happens to make too many?'

'No problem,' said John. 'He pushes the sausages back in and the pig comes out whole again on the other side!'

The visit to Ohio was certainly memorable. Another TV programme meant flying halfway across the world to New Zealand to the Mount Linton Station. There Ceri Lewis, a young man from Criccieth, was general manager. There I saw hundreds and hundreds of cattle. Coincidentally, two other young Welshmen from the Bala area were there at the time, both of them agricultural students. There they were, out on the wide-open fields, with 13,000 pedigree Aberdeen cattle, all of them calving. One student was cycling around them, while the other was tagging. The cattle were separated into huge holdings. One interesting feature was that farmers bought all their stock – including the bulls – locally, with every animal having to be comprehensively registered on paper. Bureaucracy was alive and kicking in New Zealand as well.

There were sheep, of course, to be seen everywhere. And watching the shepherds at work was an education. There they were, busily tagging, shearing, tending the lambs, castrating and dosing. The buildings were enormous, containing everything needed for the animals' care and attention. Ceri, who had graduated from the Welsh Agricultural College, was in his element. He was highly regarded as a pioneer in his field of agriculture. He was always being called out to various meetings and conferences. Yes, Welsh expertise in all kinds of areas is to be seen worldwide. There is an old saying that maintains that the best Welshman is an exiled Welshman. Having met Ceri I might well agree.

In New Zealand there were advantages not to be found in Wales: more resources and much more land. This made it possible to keep far larger flocks. Unlike us at home, no animal went to market; everything was sold on the hook. The big disadvantage was that the vastness of the place meant travelling long distances.

I found France to be totally different. For one thing, the flight there was much shorter, as was the travelling once we arrived. We went there to film three very popular continental breeds of cattle, Charolais, Limousin and Salers. One thing about foreigners – and here I include the English – is that they are far more prepared to sell than we are. In France, farmers sold their animals regularly. Another characteristic of the French is their tendency to feed you until you are full to bursting! The fare they place in front of you is so varied and in such large proportions that you could swear you are at a banquet. They always make you feel welcome. But their meals last for hours.

I visited the Limousin area itself. The province is situated in the heartland of France, a rural district dependent on farming and forestry. It is a flourishing region famous for its beef production. After around three calvings the cows are retired from breeding. Then, apart from show animals, these cows are kept in pens similar to pig pens, only far larger. There they are liberally fed. The barrens, as well as animals weighing some two tons, are then sold for something like £2,000 to £3,500.

71

We then went to see the Charolais, and what a visual feast. Large muscular beasts, every one a picture. And the bulls – some too heavy for the cows to bear them, meaning that artificial insemination was the usual practice. Seeing for myself the methods of farming out there raised one question in particular: what was the financial cost? And this question arose not just because I was a Cardi.

The Salers were different. These were milkers not unlike the Welsh Black cows. These can thrive at high altitudes, many of them producing excellent calves. These were the best I have seen for crossing with a Charolais bull. They looked old-fashioned, with bells tied around their necks. When 50 or 60 of them ambled down the hillside to be milked, the ringing of bells was deafening. Upon arrival every cow knew its place and took to its own usual pen without trouble.

Their calves, at six or seven months old, would be ushered out of their enclosure and led by the ear. They were then allowed to suckle. Often I would see a calf sucking on one teat while the machine milked the mother's other three teats. Cleanliness, perhaps, was not up to our standards. I visited one place where the farm was high on a hill and the cows entered a large fold-like enclosure where the units were pretty ancient. I never once saw anyone wash anything. The milk would enter straight into the tank. It would be enough to give our health and safety officers a seizure!

The French think the world of their farms. When

French farmers protest there are no half measures. In France farming is respected, far more so than over here. Here the public in general believe that farmers live on handouts. People need to be enlightened. In Scotland their Government is far more sympathetic to farmers, urging them on rather than holding them back. But here in Wales, prospects are horrific. It makes me wonder whether, all we will see on our hills before too long will be heather and ramblers. This is my personal opinion but it makes me livid when I see our ancient right to hunt foxes being curtailed. Hunting foxes has been a way of life for us country people for centuries and hunting undoubtedly works.

I remember once filming a man who kept pheasants. One morning we saw that a fox had managed to gain entry into the birds' sanctuary and had killed over 300 young pheasants. It had killed for the sake of killing. Some had been smothered. Foxes are rife nowadays, yet are almost a protected species.

Then there is the badger that is wreaking havoc among cattle. It spreads Bovine TB, leading to the forcible destruction of whole herds. God knows how many are culled needlessly just because one cow is suspected of suffering with TB. Indeed, it is thought that around half the number of cows culled are needlessly killed. In this so-called enlightened age, you would have thought that accurate tests could be carried out before culling cattle suspected of carrying the disease.

We in the media have to be very careful what we say. We can't always express openly what we feel. But here I can be as blunt and honest as I like.

6

Patagonia

IF YOU HAVEN'T been to Patagonia at least once in your lifetime then you haven't lived, especially if you're Welsh. Yes, it is a long and tortuous journey and can be expensive. But there are specialist travel agents in Wales now who can facilitate it for you. I was fortunate to be able to go over there twice as part of my television work. But even if I had not been that lucky, I'm sure I would have visited the place somehow or other. Going to Patagonia should be high on your list of places to visit before you die.

I first visited Patagonia with *Cefn Gwlad* in 1996. I returned four years later. Then, in 2015, on the 150th anniversary of the first landing of Welsh immigrants who sailed there on the *Mimosa*, we put together a composite documentary using excerpts from both visits.

Travelling to Patagonia is a pilgrimage. Even nowadays the journey means travelling some 7,000 miles by plane. It can take nearly 15 hours of flying to get to Buenos Aires and then a further hour and a half to Trelew and more still to Esquel. Just imagine the journey facing those early settlers. It took two months. There were about 160 souls on the *Mimosa*, with adults paying £12 per head and children at half-price. The Welsh emigration to Patagonia lasted until the beginning of the twentieth century. In Welsh, Patagonia is often referred to as 'Y Wladfa', meaning 'The Colony'.

To anyone visiting Patagonia for the first time it can prove to be a shock. It is totally different to Wales. Apart from its expanse, the first thing likely to hit you is the landscape. It varies from areas of lush growth to the arid pampas, from the flatlands of the prairie to the mighty snowcapped Andes. But what is even more striking is its vastness. Patagonia measures nearly 400,000 square miles. Compare that to Wales and its 8,000 square miles. Yet it is less populated than Wales.

As for culture shock, it is not just the fact that Welsh is widely spoken there but also the fact that the spoken Welsh is so much purer than ours. It remains untainted by Anglicized words. Add to that the Spanish intonation, Patagonian Welsh somehow sounds more exotic. It is estimated that there are some 50,000 Patagonians of Welsh descent and that between 5,000 and 12,000 speak Welsh as their first language. There are three Welsh-Spanish bilingual schools and one monolingual Welsh-language school, as well as a Welsh college. There are some 80 Welsh learners' courses attended by around a thousand people.

Not only does the language survive, but so do examples of the old Welsh way of life. When I visited Ifor and Esther Hughes near Esquel, I was amazed to see them moving their herd of Hereford cattle from their winter grazing near Tecka to their summer pastures around Lake Rosario.

This corresponds with the ancient Welsh custom of moving cattle from the winter 'hendre' to the summer 'hafod'.

To mark the 150th anniversary we used extracts from my two visits to produce a programme called *Antur yr Andes* (The Andes Adventure). I recalled the fact that I had visited what was the last generation who could remember some of the original settlers who had arrived on the *Mimosa*. Among those whom I had met in 1996 were Irfon Davies and Elmer Davies de MacDonald who lived in Tir Halen (Salt Land), Chubut. Irfon lived at Tanybryn, and when I met him he was playing a hymn tune on the organ. The words went:

Gwaed y groes sy'n codi i fyny
'Reiddil yn goncwerwr mawr.

(The blood of the cross elevates
  The weakling to a conqueror.)

Welsh hymns were not his only repertoire. He also loved playing Spanish tango music. Here and there around the place lay rusting tractors, binders and a baler, redundant remnants of his early farming days. But in a nearby field grazed a fine herd of cattle. Among them ruled the king of the herd, Jack the bull.

Irfon showed me the irrigation canals; their floodgates opened once every fortnight. Without such canals, excavated by the early settlers, the land would be as arid and unyielding as the surrounding plains.

Despite his Welsh roots, Irfon considered himself an Argentinian. His grandparents, Dafydd and Catherine Davies, had ventured across the ocean with their two children and it was at Tanybryn that Irfon's father, Robert, was born.

We retired to the house and Irfon, a bachelor, reminisced about his younger days and his craft as a farrier. He learnt it all from books, the first of which was a book written in Welsh. In the kitchen stood a large weighing scale. We had been arguing which one of us weighed the most. Now we could find out. I was a full stone heavier than Irfon.

I left Irfon and went to meet his sister Elmer, whose husband had passed away. When I arrived she was feeding the chickens. Her father had been a choir conductor and she had inherited his calling. She felt sad that her choir was much diminished in number from what it had once been. But when I arrived at choir practice, I was surprised to discover that there were some two dozen members present. Any choir conductor back in Wales would have been happy with so many members.

Elmer told me that the favourite Welsh hymn among the Patagonian Welsh was 'Calon Lân', meaning 'A Pure Heart'. She sang it for me – in Spanish. Listening to her I picked up just one Spanish word, which was 'corazón', meaning 'heart'. I then returned to see Irfon. He sang to me the hymn he had been practising earlier. I then asked him whether he had ever considered marrying. He replied that he hadn't. His reason for staying single? He loved all women! That meant, he said, sharing his love with other women apart from his wife. And that, he added, would have led to a problem. I had to agree with him.

We then visited the cemetery at Tir Halen where members of Irfon and Elmer's family are buried. There, Irfon had already bought a plot for himself and Elmer; grave Number 62, next to their parents and both sets of grandparents.

Among the highlights of my 2000 visit was meeting Vincent Evans, Melin Nant Fach, Cwm Hyfryd (Pleasant Valley), and listening to him playing the accordion and singing Dafydd Iwan's classic 'Mi Glywaf y Llais' (I Hear the Voice). The words were very appropriate and reminded me of how the early pioneers must have felt as they trekked in search for a suitable place to settle. When they reached one particular location, it is said that one of them looked around and uttered the words:

'What a pleasant valley!'

And the name stuck. Is it a true story or a part of the growing legend? Who cares. It is still known as Cwm Hyfryd. A most appropriate name. It deserves to be true. And, as Vincent sang, I saw the years roll back before my eyes.

Mi glywaf, mi glywaf y llais
Yn galw, yn galw yn glir,
A minnau ar grwydr ymhell o'm llwybr,
Ymhell o'm cynefin dir,
Yn dal i gerdded heb lygaid i weled
A'r daith yn flin ac yn hir.

(I hear, yes I hear the sweet voice
That's calling, that's calling so clear,
And I ever wandering afar from the pathway
So far from the place I belong,
Still wandering, still straying, my eyes never seeing,
The journey so tiresome and long.)

This must exactly be how those early pioneers felt as they walked and walked looking for a place to settle down where they could work and raise a family. To me, listening to Vincent was a magical moment during my travels around Patagonia.

It was then on to see Tommy Davies. I had visited Tommy in 1996 as well, when we had travelled the road over the plain from the Camwy Valley to the Andes mountains. I stopped at a farm called Hyde Park, its name painted in white on a discarded car tyre. This was Tommy's home. I knocked on the door and Tommy came out to greet me. He was 92 by then. I was immediately struck by his noble-looking moustache. He invited me in. I explained to him that I didn't have much time to spare. His answer was unexpected and shrewd:

'Dai, you've not got enough time to be in a hurry!'

Inside, the kitchen was still full of the original furniture. The dresser and other effects had either been shipped over with the family or made by them. The house itself was 120 years old. Tommy was one of two brothers who farmed there. The land had now been sold but Tommy still got up at seven o'clock each morning. I immediately took to Tommy. Like me he loved his meat. And like me he was a big eater. Sometimes for breakfast he would eat a whole ostrich egg. An ostrich egg is more than 20 times bigger than a chicken's egg. I didn't ask him how large his saucepan was.

After meeting Tommy Hyde Park, the documentary then went back to my 1996 visit when I had met Ada Griffiths from Gaiman in the Camwy Valley. There I was amazed to see so many tea houses. The tea house is a feature of Patagonian life. Ada's tea house was named Tŷ Draw i'r Avon, meaning The House Beyond the River. When I called, Ada was busy rolling dough using a century-old rolling pin that had belonged to her grandmother.

Ada, who was 86, was one of 14 children and was the second eldest. At her tea house she offered a choice of five sweet cakes. The ingredients, the milk, cream and eggs, came from the family's farm located on an exposed and windy spot up the road. Ada milked the cows once a day out in the open. I could well have been back in rural Cardiganshire a century earlier. The cows were docile, and Ada was an old hand at the chore. She had been milking regularly since she was ten. And although I hadn't milked a cow by hand for years, I helped her out. The sound of the milk hissing into the pail revived some old memories. The milk was then poured into the separator, a process that I hadn't seen for many years either. Ada turned the handle, with the separated cream then poured into a churn to be turned into butter. The butter, in turn, would be used in the mixture that made the sweet, tasty cakes in the tea house.

The next person we featured was Billy Hughes, whose roots were in Builth Wells. As noted, his parents Ifor and Esther Hughes lived near Esquel. Billy and his family lived on a new housing estate in Gaiman where he worked as a wool warehouse manager. Back on the farm in Esquel the language was always Welsh. When Billy rang home he would always converse in Welsh with his mother. And at their home in Gaiman, Billy and his wife and two children spoke Welsh. The children, however, would often answer in Spanish. According to Billy there were many potential Welsh speakers in the area but they chose not to speak the language. I told him that we had the very same problem in Wales.

Billy's work took him all over Patagonia inspecting and buying the best quality wool. The chosen wool would then be stored at the warehouse before being sold on for making woollen products. I accompanied him on one of his visits to a surprisingly fertile area, thanks to the local irrigation scheme. At the farm I watched Billy pulling out samples from woollen bales for assessing and testing. He would visit around 200 farms during the course of the year. The farm we visited kept 2,000 sheep. It was interesting for me to see four shepherds, or rather gauchos on horseback, rounding up the sheep. They reminded me of the Nantllwyd brothers on Tregaron mountain back in the 1950s.

Billy explained that there were strong campaigns by

various organisations to promote Welsh. There was one such organisation in Gaiman, where a number of locals met every Friday evening to speak the language. Billy had visited Wales four times and was making plans for another visit.

I discovered that the best time of day to be out and about in Patagonia was early morning. And it was early morning when I visited Benito Owen and Onnen Roberts. Benito, who ran a cheese factory, had his roots in the Bala area. He was quite a character. Onnen was unmarried and proud of it. She kept a newsagent's shop in Gaiman and her delightful personality had made it the most popular shop in the district. Although it was a newsagent, it stocked all kinds of other goods as well. She was a bubbly, humorous lady who had a rich turn of phrase and was right at the heart of the local Welsh community.

Milk supplies reached Benito's factory at 7.30 every morning. But, as a farmer, he would get up at four in the morning to deal with the milking. He would bring the cows in and then return them to the field on horseback. At the factory he had a staff of three. The process of producing a whole cheese took 20 days and the factory turned out a variety of cheeses.

Next I met Bobi Jones, whose family had emigrated from Rhyl. He was farming Bryn Gwyn, Gaiman, with his wife Evelyn. I met him as he returned on his tractor having been mending fences. Here again, the irrigation system pioneered by the settlers had been responsible for the farm's existence, and the same was true of the neighbouring farms. Bobi kept Hereford cattle as well as some Shorthorns. Every year Bobi would buy some 800 calves. The farm was around 100 acres and he farmed a similar sized holding nearby.

Bobi had last visited Wales in 1991. But he wouldn't want to return permanently. There were too many people in Wales, according to Bobi. Evelyn revealed that her mother hailed from the Dinas Mawddwy area, while her father's family was from Llanuwchllyn. They had two daughters and a son. Both daughters had left but the son, Oswald, was living at home in the farmhouse which dated back to 1880.

Bobi kept a flock of particularly woolly merino sheep, each animal carrying 16 kilos of wool. The wool in this case was more important than the meat.

Bobi needed to harvest some alfalfa, so I joined him. We were immediately attacked by a swarm of mosquitoes that bit like rabid Jack Russells. I swear that Patagonian mosquitoes were larger than our swallows! It reminded me of my earlier visit to Gaiman when I met the Penderyn sisters, Sandra and Ingrid, and their mother, Owena Day. I called at the chemist's shop run by Sandra. I asked her for mosquito repellent, adding, 'They're eating me alive!' Her retort was: 'We'd need a lot of mosquitoes to eat you, Dai Jones!'

Cheeky! The Penderyn family still cooked in the traditional way of the early settlers, using an old-fashioned stone oven out in the garden. There, according to Sandra, they would 'cook rice pudding for nice people!'

We lingered awhile at a place named Pant y March, meaning the Hollow of the Stallion. According to tradition, when the early pioneers arrived they encountered a wild stallion there. Whether the story is true or not is again unimportant. I'd like to think it is.

Next on the documentary was Emrys Jenkins from Tir Halen. It was a scorching hot day, with Emrys and his sons busily branding and tagging calves. Emrys had few opportunities to speak Welsh. Neither his wife nor his sons could speak it. So following his marriage in 1957 he'd had little reason to do so. The only opportunities he had of conversing in Welsh was when he visited his mother or talked to her on the phone. Prior to my visit he hadn't spoken a word of Welsh for three years. Yet his language as he talked to me was both fluent and pure.

Emrys grew crops of Indian corn, pumpkins and potatoes by the ton, all for the family's consumption. I had long waited for a chance to attend an *asado*, an open-air barbecue of roast meat, and Emyr provided it. What a feast!

Some have accused me of double standards regarding my admiration for the Welsh Patagonians. I have been chided for praising them while condemning settlers who have imposed themselves on communities in other countries, including English incomers to Wales. But there is a big difference. The Welsh did not impose themselves upon the native Patagonians. No, the Welsh were invited by an Argentine Government that encouraged foreign settlers to areas of the country where the population was sparse. The Welsh were allocated 100 square miles of land in the Chubut Valley. It was, however, arid land, and the early pioneers were forced to wander around searching for a suitable place to settle. Undoubtedly, they were venturesome and brave. But they were *invited* to Patagonia. As for immigration into Wales, we have no choice.

Looking back at my two visits to Patagonia, what will always remain in my memory will not only be the fact that the Welsh language has endured, but that it is spoken so purely by people like Emrys Tir Halen. Yes, it is surprising that it has survived at all. But the fact that it is spoken so fluently and so correctly is nothing short of miraculous. There the language has not been contaminated by another stronger language.

I feel privileged to have visited Patagonia and to have met and conversed with the descendants of the early Welsh settlers. I will never forget Patagonia for as long as I live.

7

This land is my land

THE POET EIFION Wyn, well over a century ago, wrote a verse that is still relevant. He argued that it was worth becoming an exile sometimes so that he could then return and love Wales even more. Sentimental? Yes. Clichéd? Yes. But true.

It is certainly true in my case. Over the past 20 years my travels have continued. To Europe, New Zealand and Patagonia you can add Canada. Yes, I have been fortunate in being able to see some of the wonders of the world. But the greatest wonders are here at my feet.

I have often been asked for my favourite place in Wales. I have no hesitation in declaring that the place nearest to my heart is Montgomeryshire. I have received a princely welcome in every county in Wales but nowhere can compare to Montgomeryshire. There is something about the place, something you just can't explain. For one thing, its inhabitants don't seem to be in too much of a hurry. There is time for everything. Time enough to think. Time enough to act. There is never a need to rush.

Some of my most memorable programmes were filmed

in Montgomeryshire. Among them were those about the lives of William and Richard Cae'r Berllan and Don Garreg Ddu. The area is a virtual treasure-trove of old customs and idiomatic adages. Usually, when I discuss farming, it always ends up with economics. Not so with people such as these. And their unique accent – I love listening to it. Whenever I have visited the area for an eisteddfod, a concert or a market, I have always felt a kinship, a warmth that I have never felt anywhere else.

Topography or landscape has always been integral to *Cefn Gwlad*. What the viewers see is often just as important as what they hear; otherwise they might as well be listening to the radio. And as far as the landscape goes, my most memorable programme was one we filmed not in Montgomeryshire, as it happens, but rather in neighbouring Meirionethshire.

I'm not very adept at anything physical. But filming this programme involved walking 12 miles between the two Aran mountains, Aran Fawddwy and Aran Benllyn, from Llanymawddwy to Llanuwchllyn. It was early spring and the landscape was already reawakening. I began my trek at Cwm Cywarch near Dinas Mawddwy. It was easy to imagine this remote valley isolated for weeks under winter snow. Before setting off I called at Plas Penbont, the home of twins Beti and Robat Williams. Beti was out in the field milking one of the pair's Welsh Blacks. It was like stepping out of the TARDIS and into an earlier age. Beti tended and milked the cows while Robat looked after the sheep. As Beti milked one of the cows and Robat looked on, we were dwarfed by the towering Aran mountains above us. Beti drew upon her store of local knowledge and folklore. She recited a poem that I had never heard before:

Gwnes destun cân eleni
I Aran Fawddwy fawr,
I ddangos sut un ydi,
Mi draethaf i chwi nawr,
Mae'n fynydd ar ben mynydd
Yn uchel iawn i'r nen,
A llawer o hen Gymry
Sy'n hoffi mynd i'w phen.

(I sang a song this year
To Aran Fawddwy tall,
To tell you what it looks like,
I'll now describe it all,
It's a mountain upon a mountain
Reaching the very sky,
And many are the Welsh people
Who love to climb that high.)

Although Plas Penbont must be one of the remotest crofts in Wales, Beti and Robat were accustomed to seeing strangers passing by, mostly ramblers. They weren't a problem, said Beti. According to Robat they followed the Countryside Code, keeping to the designated paths.

The path I was to take was a familiar one for the twins. They had walked all these paths since childhood. The main path leads to Drws-y-nant and Rhyd-y-main. In the opposite direction the nearest village was Dinas Mawddwy. Dolgellau was the nearest town, where Robat would visit the sheep sale every Friday. The twins lived a simple life. They had no luxuries of any kind. Indeed, following my visit, they went to Tywyn to buy a television set so that they could watch themselves on *Cefn Gwlad*.

Being with Beti and Robat reminded me of another *Cefn Gwlad* programme from the first ever series. Back then we filmed another brother and sister, Huw and Catrin Pugh, Cwm Ffernol, near Pennal. They were also a good example of a generation that had largely disappeared. Before we started filming the cows, we were ordered by Miss Pugh to empty our pockets of any cigarettes and leave them on the kitchen table. We were not allowed to smoke in the cowshed as it could harm the health of Siani, her favourite cow. Miss Pugh had named every cow and sheep kept on the croft.

I was to be guided along the path between the two Arans by Richard Davies, the seasonal warden. The weather was set fine which wasn't all good news, for walkers like us faced 12 miles of toil. There would be, thankfully, a breeze on the upper slopes. That, at least, was my hope. I prayed for the rain to keep away.

The natural starting point was Cwm Cywarch where Beti and Robat lived. We set off and soon met up with Hedd Puw at Blaen y Cwm who was ushering his flock of newly shorn sheep. On this rocky terrain, rounding up sheep had to be a difficult task. This was where his wife's family had lived, and Hedd, his wife and their two sons, Dewi and Owain, had settled there four years previously.

By the time I had finished chatting with Hedd, I had some catching up to do. Richard was way ahead. We all have our weaknesses and mine is my tendency to gossip which, in turn, always makes me dawdle. I caught up with Richard at a rock named Craig Camddwr, and by now I was sweating in the warmth of the sun. We reached a large patch of ferns and I remembered an old verse:

Aeth Wil Rhydyfro
I hela ryw dro
Ond mi gollodd ei ffordd yn y rhedyn.

(Wil Rhydyfro
 A-hunting did go
 But he lost his way in the ferns.)

I hoped I wouldn't suffer the same fate as Wil. Onwards and upwards we climbed. I couldn't help noticing how worn the path was, evidence of how popular it was with walkers. The only sound to break the silence was the bleating of sheep calling for their lambs. I was surprised to see so much evidence of mountain land being adapted for farming. Again, I was to appreciate the difficulties facing shepherds when gathering their flocks. I imagined they would need a few helpers, as well as dogs. By now my chest was wheezing, especially when negotiating the high stiles over the stone boundary walls.

It was good to learn from Richard that the relationship between the local farmers and the National Park officials was a happy one. We reached a rock named Craig Cywarch. How insignificant it had looked from the valley. Up close it was huge. Running in another direction was a trail known as Llywelyn's Path. I wondered at the historical significance of the name. We were now completely alone, with not another soul in sight. And Richard expounded on the difference between the two words 'loneliness' and 'solitude'. This was solitude.

I was now so hungry; my stomach must have thought that my throat had been cut. On we went through the ferns and the sparse grass. But there were signs of a good crop of whinberries come summer's end.

Parts of the path needed maintenance. The main enemy, according to Richard, was running water. It eroded the surface. We reached the summit of Cywarch and the boundary of two farms, Rhos y Bont and Blaen Cywarch. I now felt firmer ground underfoot. The path ahead was clear and I could see Aran Fawddwy on the distant horizon. Cotton grass danced around us in the wind. I was surprised at the compactness of the ground but Richard assured me that it would be boggy come wintertime. Small birds flitted around, but no grouse were to be seen any longer.

On we walked, with me ruing the fact that God hadn't blessed me with longer legs. Unfortunately, he had given me legs that were too short and a tongue that was too long! By now my lungs were wheezing like a pair of bellows. Then the sun broke through the clouds revealing a panorama that would beautifully grace any landscape painter's canvas.

Then, suddenly, I stumbled upon something completely unexpected. There in front of me were the remains of a plane, a de Havilland Mosquito, that had collided with the side of the mountain on 9 February 1944, killing the whole crew. There were parts of the plane scattered around like flotsam. And on one piece someone had painted the stark words, 'NO SURVIVORS'.

On we trudged, the journey getting harder. And I remembered a rhyme that Beti Williams had recited:

Roedd rhyw hen wraig yn brwyno
Ar ochr Bwlch y Groes,
Am fynd i ben yr Aran
Am unwaith yn ei hoes,
Ac ar ôl mynd i fyny
Ac edrych ar i lawr
Ni chredai neb cyn hynny
Fod yr hen fyd mor fawr.

(An old maid cutting rushes
At Bwlch y Groes one day,
Who'd never climbed the Aran
Finally got her way,

She reached the very summit
And looking down did see
Why no-one seemed to realise
How big this world could be.)

Before reaching the crest I had to stop to draw breath
– for two reasons. One because of my exertions, the other
because the sight took away what little was left of my
breath. Below me was the Drysgol ridge and the source of
the river Dyfi. The horizon had become a gigantic circle that
encompassed both Snowdonia to the north and the Brecon
Beacons to the south. I was reminded of Dewi Emrys' stanza
to the 'Horizon', a verse that is regarded as a classic:

Wele rith fel ymyl rhod – o'n cwmpas,
    Campwaith dewin hynod.
  Hen linell bell nad yw'n bod,
  Hen derfyn nad yw'n darfod.

It is impossible to translate it in verse and harmony,
a form of poetry that is unique to the Welsh language.
Roughly it translates like this:

Lo! A mirage like a wheel's rim – around me,
    A masterpiece by a strange wizard.
  A far-off outline that doesn't exist,
  An extremity that's never-ending.

Richard reeled off the names of some of the landmarks below us, among them Cadair Bronwen (Bronwen's Seat) and Cadair y Berwyn (The Berwyns' Seat). As we reached the summit I was amazed at the thousands of small stones that littered the crest. Yes, this was solitude alright. A place to rest one's soul. I could see Llangadfan in the far distance, as well as Cwm Nant yr Eira and Y Foel. Some of the songs of my youth came back to mind, songs that I had sung at eisteddfods and concerts, sentimental songs of farming and shepherding. And there, on the Aran, I sang one of them with no-one save Richard and the various creatures of nature listening to me.

Then, the performance over, we were joined on the summit by Trefor Esgair-clawdd and his sheepdog. We were standing at the boundary of his farm, hence the significance of the name Esgair-clawdd, meaning Ridgebank. Trefor would climb up to the ridge once a fortnight to keep an eye on his flock. It meant negotiating, of course, a steep climb. No vehicle could ascend these slopes, not even a pony could manage it. Trefor would leave his sheep on the mountain over the winter months, save for those that were lambing, and they would be driven down a fortnight before giving birth. Nearby stood a huge stone outcrop known as Y Fuwch Ddu (The Black Cow). Close-up it did not look anything like a cow but Trefor assured me that from a distance, caught at a certain angle by the rays of the sun, it did look exactly like a black cow.

Trefor revealed that local farmers had formed a society

to protect the two Aran mountains. And he scorned the idea of people travelling overseas to see the wonders of the world. He wouldn't swap this landscape for any view in any land. I couldn't but agree with him. I now realised why so many walkers and ramblers were attracted to this remarkable spot. Richard reminded me that it was, for him, an attraction he saw daily. And he welcomed visitors with open arms. He could not think why he should deprive other people of the pleasures he himself enjoyed so much.

Between the two Aran mountains is Aran Fach, the Lesser Aran. Here I noticed different growing conditions and fewer stones and boulders. And there, among the vegetation, grew a plant called Corn Carw'r Mynydd. But there was no time to dawdle and on we walked. Five miles later and we could see Aran Benllyn ahead. I uttered a silent prayer. Not for the beauty of the place but because our journey was almost over. We reached Wal Lwyd (Grey Wall) with its connections to the lawless Gwylliaid Cochion Mawddwy (Red Bandits of Mawddwy), a gang of red-headed highwaymen who terrorised the area in the sixteenth century. On the summit stood some stones that reminded me of the Eisteddfod Gorsedd Circle.

From here on it would be downhill. But not before examining a cairn on the summit that had grown steadily over the years as walkers followed the custom of adding to the heap, stone by stone.

Richard and I sat by the cairn to reflect, and in my

case to enjoy a rare chance to breathe. I was now nearer to heaven than I had been for some time. Five miles to go and Bala lake looked like a duck pond down below, while the road from Dolgellau to Bala was but a long narrow ribbon. How I licked my lips in anticipation of tea in Llanuwchllyn!

On the way down we chanced upon Jac Nant Barcud and his wife Gwenfair. Jac was a member of the famous choir Côr Godre'r Aran, while Gwenfair was a member of the Uwchllyn ladies' choir. Jac kept three dozen Welsh rams and I helped him and the boys herd them. Jac had been born and bred here, and now he and Gwenfair had two boys and a girl of school age to carry on the tradition. I inspected his herd of Welsh Blacks, some crossed with Charolais. Jac had only been overseas twice, both times with the choir to the USA and Canada. But while he was away, not a day had gone by without him longing for the Arans. No, there was nowhere for Jac like Aran Benllyn.

On our descent we hurried, before the weather turned, to meet one of the area's great characters. For once we caught Dewi Talardd at home. Usually he would have been out somewhere driving his three-wheeled car. Dewi's dog Harri followed us into the house and slumped at his master's feet in front of a roaring log fire. Dewi considered the kitchen fire as his 'number one necessity', especially in winter.

Dewi had been employed by the Forestry Commission and his greatest delight was mechanics or, as he said, 'fiddling around with old engines'. His house had no mains electricity. Dewi had built his own electrical generating system from bits of scrap discarded by others.

Dewi hated bureaucrats that made his life hell. According to Dewi every bureaucrat should be placed on the dole. He hated the modern life dependent on cars. Motor cars had destroyed society. The Aran, on the other hand, was constant and unchanged. What had changed were the people who lived there. Yet, he would never contemplate moving away. He remembered the old Welsh adage of 'he that is born in hell, in hell he wishes to remain'. Not that the Aran was hell. No, to Dewi it was heaven.

Onward and downward we went and suddenly I was taken back half a century as I watched Simon Jones, Tan-y-bwlch, cutting peat. This wasn't merely staged for the camera, it was still a way of life for Simon. He had been cutting peat since he was a lad of 15. Indeed, he had not only burnt peat at home but had supplied neighbours as well. However, nowadays he cut and harvested just one load for his own use. What with the peat, a few hundredweights of coal and a pile of logs, he had enough fuel to last him all through the winter.

Simon's family had lived here for generations. He had evidence that showed his ancestors living here in 1707. Simon had attended the local primary and secondary school in Bala but chose to leave the latter early to work as a shepherd. He became restless and went to live in England, but he only stayed there for one winter. The call of the Aran was too strong.

Our next call was Wern Fawr where we met up with Arwyn Roberts. When we arrived he was preparing to ferry fencing material up to the high slopes. For this purpose he had bought an eight-wheeled vehicle called the Hill Farmer. I was given the opportunity to drive it. Luckily I didn't need to reverse it!

Alongside the house was a much more primitive tractor, the Marshall, that dated back to 1936. It had been used for contracting out in past times and was now being driven by Tommy Roberts. It had cost £600 even in those days and had arrived by train at Dolgellau station. The old Marshall was a familiar sight in the area, its loud popping sound echoing everywhere. We attempted to start it. I turned the starting handle and, after much coaxing, the engine eventually burst into life. For those living miles around, its popping must have rolled back the years.

Next we called with Dei Rhyd-sarn, a confirmed bachelor, a busy farmer and a member of the Aran choir. When I called he was ushering calves to pasture in order to fatten them. They would then be sold at market, either in St Asaph or Oswestry.

Having finished that task he started fencing, going at it hammer and tongs as if he was being paid by the hour. The fence would confine sheep brought down from the Aran. Later they would be sold at Bala market. Although a faithful member of the choir, he wasn't able to join his fellow choristers on foreign tours as he had no-one to deputise for him on the farm. Now I was his helper, running here and there to fetch staples, the sledgehammer or the crowbar. Dei well remembered the old custom of driving sheep onto the Aran during the summer months and then driving them down again before winter.

It was there at Rhyd-sarn that my journey ended, one that had given me the rare opportunity of meeting all those special people who lived and worked between Aran Fawddwy and Aran Benllyn. It involved a lot of walking and much sweating. But to someone carrying so much weight it wasn't all bad. I had traversed one of the most memorable places created by God. Yes, a place for resting the soul.

8

A life that's full

To RETURN TO Sinatra and 'My Way'. The song includes the line, 'I've lived a life that's full'. That is also true of my own life. It has been – and is – not only full but also fulfilling. In other words, I love every aspect of my work.

Often, while out filming *Cefn Gwlad* as the presenter – and latterly as producer as well – I feel privileged. Not everyone can claim that they are paid for doing what they love the most. I do feel an element of guilt, not that it persists very long in someone who is an out-and-out Cardi!

But that is what *Cefn Gwlad* is to me. I love relating the enjoyment I get from my job to the viewers. One of the joys of working on the series is the opportunity to visit various places throughout Wales and beyond. Often the pleasure I feel doesn't end with the filming. Indeed, time and again, there is even more delight in being able to relax away from the camera with local people over a cup of tea or a pint afterwards. I can then hear local characters' experiences more intimately, some of their secrets even, and feel a part of the neighbourhood. At times like these, work and pleasure become one.

Every time I go out filming I feel that I am a part of another world, a different world. Even before the filming starts, work on the TV series entails travelling around looking for subjects, be they characters, events or interesting localities. Each person and every neighbourhood has their character or characteristics. Look for them and you will find them. As the Bible states: 'Ask, and it shall be given you; seek, and ye shall find; knock, and it shall be opened unto you.' And that to me is the greatest privilege: being able to meet people in their own neighbourhoods, either on camera or away from the reach of the lens.

Sometimes *Cefn Gwlad* provides a bonus in combining more than one of my interests. This happened in 2010 with a programme featuring farming and singing. In the company of 'Hogia Bryniog', the Bryniog brothers, we were able to amalgamate farming, singing and their love for their neighbourhood.

The Bryniog family from Melin-y-coed near Llanrwst is remarkable. There are five brothers, all of them singers, plus one sister. Although their surname is Davies, they are invariably referred to as the Bryniog family, after the name of their home, Bryniog Uchaf.

The boys are Tom, Jack, Dai, Arthur and Gwilym and the sister is called Ann. Tom was the first to gain fame when he won the Blue Ribband at the National Eisteddfod for singing William Walton's cantata 'Belshazzar's Feast'. Hearing Tom sing invariably sends shivers down my spine. When Tom sings 'Cân yr Arad Goch' (The Song of the Red

Plough), he not only sings the words, but lives by them as a busy and conscientious farmer.

Following his Blue Ribband success in 1980, he was deluged with invitations to appear on stage throughout Wales and beyond. At eisteddfods Tom was virtually unbeatable on the oratorio. At the Bala National Eisteddfod in 1997 he sang D. Pughe Evans' 'Brad Dynrafon' (Dunravon's Betrayal) so clearly that even the sheep grazing on the Aran must have lifted their heads to listen.

All the brothers are baritones, save for Arthur who is a tenor. Jack is recognised as the finest musician in the family. All five have been members of various choirs at one time or another.

Dai was the brother who featured foremost in the TV documentary. He is, in fact, a remarkable talker, his language both erudite and clear as a bell. According to Dai, who farmed Gorsedd Drycin farm, Arthur, the second eldest, was the 'lump of clay' their father fashioned into a true musician. Arthur learnt sol-fa early in life and went on to win a host of prizes. He, said Dai, was the spur that drove Tom to succeed at the top.

Jack, according to Dai, was the quietest. But, he added, the calmer the river, the deeper its flood. Jack was a pianist and a musician from head to toe. He would coach local children for their appearances at concerts and especially for singing Christmas carols.

Dai himself came next. He had little to say about

himself. Rather, he turned to the next in line, Gwilym. He was married and had moved to farm Maes y Pandy in Abergynolwyn and he also did some work for a local vet. He was a member of the Dyfi Male Voice Choir. He now lives back in his old neighbourhood.

Ann, the youngest of the six, is the only sister and she lives near Bala.

'If it hadn't been for Ann, there may well have been 20 of us boys,' said Dai. 'Lucky she arrived when she did!'

Ann may have been the princess among the princes, but there was no doubting who was the Bryniog queen. She still lived nearby in a cottage named Bwthyn Bryniog.

'Our mother was always the backbone of the family,' said Dai. 'But she refused to be treated any different to anyone else in our home. I just can't fathom how she managed with all of us. She coped without any outside help, neither with the household chores nor with the farm work. She reckoned that her greatest blessing was when father bought a washing machine.'

I left Dai for the time being and went to meet the eldest brother, Tom. He was busy building a stone wall. He was glad to see me as it gave him an excuse to down tools and guide me around the village. The chapel and the adjoining vestry were at the heart of the little village which nestles in the Conwy Valley. It was here that the family had worshipped over the years. It was here that Tom had sung in public for the very first time. He well remembered his knees trembling as he faced the audience. He still remembered the accompanist, David Jones, who had to play the introduction two or three times before the nervous little boy was confident enough to begin.

Tom recalled his first day at the local primary school, Ysgol Nant y Rhiw. There, he alleged, he only learnt how to misbehave! After only a year he was moved to Llanrwst school. He pointed out a house that had once been a shop, one of two village shops. Here at Siop Ucha, the shopkeeper had been Joni Jones, or Uncle Joni. Joni, said Tom, had another string to his bow. This was literally true. Despite losing the fingers of his left hand in a childhood accident, he became an accomplished pianist and adapted a fiddle so that he could hold the bow with his left hand while pressing the strings with his right hand. Joni Jones had been Tom's inspiration.

Back at Tom's home at Plas Bryniog, one of his sheepdogs, Llew, was slumbering in the warmth of an early summer's day. And suddenly I found myself helping Tom with the task of building his stone wall. As I watched him placing those rough stones in place, I realised that he was a craftsman as well as a singer. He explained to me that Llew was descended from a rich breed of reddish-coloured sheepdogs the family had kept for years. The dogs of this particular lineage were hardy creatures, and could run and work all day. Tom showed me a litter that had only just been born. I fancied one of them but, unfortunately, they had all been promised. I would have to wait for the next litter.

As well as farming Plas Bryniog, Tom rented land higher up on the mountain and here he kept cattle over the summer months. He took me up there to land located just below Moel Siabod which was owned by Gwilym Jones, or Gwilym Rhos as he is better known. As he drove me there he sang a patriotic Welsh song about Llywelyn, the last Prince of Wales. So expressive was the song that I expected to see the prince himself thundering past on his noble steed.

Here we touched on a feature that often crops up on *Cefn Gwlad*. Tom and I started comparing our different dialects. I have always respected differing dialects. They are, to me, as important as the language itself. I am known for slipping into whatever dialect is spoken in the areas I visit. I tossed around words like 'esgair' (ridge) and 'gwellt y bwla' (purple moor-grass), while Tom replied with words like 'cawnen' (reed) and 'crawc', another name for moor-grass.

I interviewed all the brothers individually and one of the most intriguing conversations was when Dai spoke of his father's influence on the family. The most important piece of furniture at Bryniog, according to the father, wasn't the dresser, the corner cupboard or the grandfather clock. No, it was the piano. John Davies was also a pioneer in his farming methods and was way ahead of his time. Long before the pioneering research led by Moses Griffith and Llew Phillips at Pwllpeiran, Cwmystwyth, and similar research into mountain farming by Captain Bennett Evans on the slopes of Eisteddfa Gurig, John Davies had been quietly developing his own methods.

Dai would turn his cattle onto the mountain, feeding them with silage in the morning and with grass in the afternoon. He adopted many of the methods pioneered by his father. For example, he wasn't one for ploughing but he was a great believer in spreading lime on land. Dai maintained that John Davies had left his sons and daughter a legacy based on three endowments. One was the Welsh alphabet, which Dai reeled off with ease (not many Welsh people can do this nowadays). The second was sol-fa. And the third was recognising the ownership of sheep from their earmarks. Through imparting such knowledge, his father had opened gates for the children. What a turn of phrase. I will long remember Dai's rich vocabulary and his original idioms.

I thoroughly enjoyed meeting the Bryniog family. This is the kind of television programme that makes someone proud to be in the business of entertaining and enlightening viewers. In this documentary I felt that we succeeded in combining the brothers' various daily activities against the backdrop of a unique Hiraethog mountain landscape, with Tom's songs of Llywelyn and other historical Welsh warriors woven into it all. Dafydd Iwan has a classic song, 'Yma o Hyd', meaning 'Still Here'. It is an anthem to the perseverance of the Welsh nation and its language. It could well have been composed with the Bryniog family in mind.

*

As we travel around from location to location I continually learn and discover more and more, not only of the present but also of the past. In fact, much of Welsh history is relevant to the present day. Typical was the programme we filmed at Berain, Llannefydd, home of John and Eirian Jones and their children, Elin, Ifan, Jacob and Elias. All four children were of school age but they also helped out on the farm. Also very much involved were John's parents, Richard and Iona. The name 'Berain' is synonymous with one of the most colourful and controversial women in Welsh history, Catrin of Berain. The present family still live in the small fourteenth-century mansion situated in picturesque countryside.

It is now a dairy farm where the family keep a 200-strong head of cattle. Richard keeps Friesians, including a few bulls, but as the herd expanded he decided to turn to artificial insemination. Every individual cow's yield was meticulously recorded on a computer in the milking parlour.

Around us were acre upon acre of lush accessible fields stretching between Clocaenog and St Asaph. We then visited the family's second farm, Maes y Brwyn, where wheat and oats grew in profusion, enough to provide for the stock with more left over to sell. I also had the opportunity to admire their herds of Welsh and Texel sheep.

I had the chance to chat with Elwyn Griffiths who, true to the tradition of a faithful servant, had worked there for some 40 years. I then joined Iona at the local place of worship, Capel Cefn Berain. Written prominently above the pulpit was the phrase, 'Duw cariad yw' (God is love). The chapel was built to seat 100 but there were only 30 members by now. Yes, a story that is common throughout Wales these days.

It was Iona who enlightened me on the story of Catrin of Berain. She was reputedly the first woman in Wales to be accepted at the same level in society as menfolk. She had four husbands, all prominent men and all of them rich. There were rumours that some of them had been murdered by Catrin but, Iona reassured me, these accusations were groundless. Her character was probably blackened by men who were jealous of her success and reputation. Women in the sixteenth century were not influential, so a story had to be created to explain her success. Her four marriages resulted in six children and 32 grandchildren. That accounts, perhaps, for her being dubbed 'Mother of Wales'.

As I looked around I found it hard to believe that this lady had once owned 3,000 acres of the surrounding countryside and earned an income of £100 per annum. Unfortunately, her grave at Llannefydd cemetery is unmarked. There, as I contemplated the success of Catrin who died in 1591, the modern age caught up with me as Berain's modern machinery moved past me as they reaped the harvest of the Clwyd Valley.

*

For all the appeal of visiting foreign parts, I get the same thrill when I visit countries closer to home, be they Scotland or Ireland. Crossing Offa's Dyke to England does not have quite the same feel, probably because it is so close. But there are relevant stories there as well. Recently I crossed the border to Herefordshire to meet a most interesting Welshman. He was Humphrey Davies, known as Wmffre, or to accord him his full name, Dafydd Wmffre Williams Davies.

Hereford boasts a cathedral and so is regarded a city. And it has close links with Wales, not only geographically but also historically and commercially. Owain Glyndŵr attacked Hereford. And the weekly market attracts scores of Welsh people from across the border.

Wmffre was not a newcomer. He remembers first visiting Hereford on 24 September 1979. How come he knows the date so accurately? He was on a Sunday school trip with members of Capel y Fadfa chapel, Talgarreg, near Llandysul. The date is still imprinted on his memory. He liked the place so much that he later returned there to work at the Wyevale Garden Centre, and before long he was a senior gardener there.

Wmffre was a former farmer who was used to growing vegetables. He remembered the old custom at summer's end when he, his two brothers and their father, would harvest swedes. Wmffre's interest in gardening came about because, as a youngster, he argued so much with his brothers that his father banished him to work in the garden. This kindled his interest in plants. He recalled that the farm grew enough vegetables to feed the family all year round.

When organic gardening took hold and became fashionable in recent times, Wmffre wasn't all that surprised as this was the method his family had always adhered to. And it was the best method, he said. Farmers in times gone by were much closer to the soil when it came to deciding where and when to sow or reap.

The Wyevale Garden Centre had some 400 acres of land and employed some 200 staff. There were 30 Massey Ferguson tractors and 70 trailers to help them. Wmffre's work, although lasting all year, was seasonal in its nature. Saplings, for instance, could only be uprooted between November and March. Potted plants, on the other hand, were sold all year round.

Wyevale is one of the largest gardening centre companies in the UK and has all the latest machinery and equipment, including a device for potting plants. All that was needed was for a plant to be placed in a pot manually and then a machine filled it with soil. The filled planted pots were then placed on a conveyor belt and received by another member of staff at the other end. This work continued for 12 hours a day, six days a week.

Wmffre spent the first ten years working outdoors at Wyevale, tending to the plants and watering them before they were moved inside to be sold. Then, he said, he received the DCM. No, not the Distinguished Conduct Medal but rather 'Don't Come back Monday'! But he was reprieved and given a job indoors at Wyevale. This meant diversifying from tending plants to selling them to the public. Twice he was appointed to be in charge of Wyevale's stand at the Chelsea Flower Show, helping visitors with their queries.

Two million plants are grown annually at Wyevale and Wmffre has, over the years, worked in every department. Four thousand plants a day can be processed there, with workers tidying and labelling plants as they move on to be placed on carts and taken to various counters for viewing.

Wmffre had only meant to spend a year at Wyevale, just for the experience. But he became a long-standing member of staff. He emphasised the need to water plants regularly. Plants were thirsty, he said, almost as thirsty as he was! But Wmffre wasn't personally satisfied with water. Not in the heart of cider country! He remembered as a lad in Talgarreg his father giving him half a crown to buy a flagon of Woodpecker Cider at the local pub. Having drunk it, he would take back the empty flagon and receive sixpence in return. Little did he think back then that he would, years later, be living and working in the very place where Woodpecker Cider is brewed by Bulmers.

We were, of course, surrounded by orchards, and every farm at one time brewed its own cider. There are more cider apple orchards in Herefordshire than there are in any other county of the UK. As senior gardener, Wmffre was well versed in his knowledge of apple varieties and their various tastes. He showed me two kinds, Michelin and Dabinett.

Herefordshire's apples were sent to cider makers such as Bulmers, Magners and Gaymers.

The countryside around us was covered with golden wheat. Here it was more profitable to grow grain than to fatten livestock such as lambs or calves. The locals were rather insular, according to Wmffre, and rather slow in accepting incomers. But he had been fully adopted as 'a Welsh-speaking Herefordshire man and a cider drinker'. It also helped that he was an avid supporter of Hereford Rugby Club. In fact, it was the warmth shown to him by the club's supporters that had made him stay in the area for so long. For 20 years he had been in charge of one of the club's teams and he was honoured for his services to English rugby. Quite an achievement for a Welshman! He was later asked to run the second XV team. He refused. Why? The club passed a new rule which meant he wouldn't be allowed to swear! Political correctness deprived him of the honour.

He had first caught the rugby bug as a schoolboy at Llandysul Grammar School where he played blindside wing-forward for three seasons. Indeed, he was team captain during his last season. He remembers begging his father to buy him a pair of rugby boots. His father agreed on condition that his son clear ferns from a hillside. He did, and then hitch-hiked to Aberystwyth, bought the new boots and caught the bus home.

A cattle market is held in Hereford every Wednesday. We attended the event and saw, naturally, Hereford cattle, all of them gloriously fat. The breed, said Wmffre, was ideal for enduring any weather conditions, be it frost or warmth. No wonder their progeny are to be found worldwide. It is estimated that there are some five million Hereford cattle in over 50 countries today.

At the market we also took a stroll through the fruit and vegetable area. Herefordshire apples are not confined to the cider variety. In the market we saw eating and cooking apples as well. Wmffre could reel off their names with ease. No wonder – in his garden he had ten different varieties, while at the garden centre he sold 31 different cultivars.

We also viewed the famous Hereford Bull statue outside The Old House (now renamed the Black and White House museum) in the city centre. It was sculpted and cast by Brian Alabaster. But, according to Wmffre, it was flawed. Its head should be white, like any worthwhile Hereford bull.

Wmffre's interest in sport wasn't just confined to rugby. He was an expert at Pétanque, a game very popular in France. It resembles bowls, except that you toss the ball towards the jack rather than roll it. Another difference is that it is played on a gravel surface rather than on grass. Wmffre challenged me to a game. I didn't let on that I had played it before on one of my visits to France. Believe it or not, but I won!

Wmffre had a dream. He intended planting 14 oak trees on Esgair, the family farm in Wales, one to remember each close relative. On the farm there are the remains of an old Norman fort, known as Castell Hwmffre (Humphrey's

Castle). The oaks would be planted there, with his relatives' names beneath them, starting with his father. Roots were all-important to Wmffre, and not only tree roots. There was evidence that his great-great-great-grandfather, who was born in 1760, had been a member at the Old Chapel in Llwynrhydowen. Then, in 1876, the local squire, staunch Tory John Lloyd, locked the chapel doors against the members and their preacher Gwilym Marles because of their Unitarian radicalism. The worshippers were not defeated. They kept meeting beneath a nearby oak tree. When the squire died the parishioners were handed back their chapel. Gwilym Marles, by the way, was Dylan Thomas' great-uncle.

Wmffre's plan was already under way. He had chosen the 14 trees. He admitted that his motive was an attempt to try to ease his longing for home. Although an exile since the late 1970s, the 'hiraeth' persisted. His message was that you can never separate a man from his roots, be they oak tree roots or family roots.

'They will still be there when I am long gone,' said Wmffre. 'And they will still be growing for centuries to come.'

9

In deep waters

MY AVERSION TO cats is well documented. Another of my pet hates is water. In my previous autobiography I tried to explain the reasons for my revulsion of both. Here I will confine my explanation to the latter. My fear of being involved with water – in it, beneath it or anywhere near it – is all too real. Or rather, *was* too real. Thanks to a challenge in the three-episode series, *Dai yn y Dŵr* (Dai in the Water), I did manage to overcome my apprehension. And I was largely successful. And now I can at least cross a bridge without panicking!

It was the Cardiff-based Boomerang TV company that was responsible for the production, with Cleif Harpwood directing. The whole purpose of the series was to try to teach me to swim, thereby conquering my fear of water. I was given a seven-day deadline. That wasn't long, considering I had tried to avoid water all my life. I consoled myself with the knowledge that God had created the world in six days. Not bad going. He rested on the seventh. I was worried, however, that my challenge would depend not on a deadline but rather on a lifeline.

We all have our trepidations. My aversion to water is

considerably lower down the scale than my fear of cats. But it had always been there, at the back of my mind. I had been on water before, and even in water – more often than not the hot variety. Not always had I been immersed intentionally. But, unlike my fear of cats, my fear of water was based on reverential respect.

Entering a swimming pool had always been an ordeal for me. To wade in slowly... but get deeper step by step... the water creeps up my shins... I advance slowly and it reaches my knees... then it creeps up my thighs... and then it reaches – you know where I mean – and I catch my breath. That, at least, was my experience.

And as for swimming, well, it is an alien activity to me. God gave me one means of moving around. He provided me with legs for walking. I have inherited my father's short legs. My mother's legs were even shorter. At our shop in London she had to climb on a box to be able to reach the bacon.

As far as I'm concerned I have enough to do when I operate my legs on dry land. In water I used to feel that my feet had no purpose when I touched the bottom. I would panic. I felt like a tractor with its wheels spinning. I would then try to use my arms. But with me, the parts of my body that always sank first were the lightest parts, my legs. My substantial belly was a great help for buoyancy. But I still had this feeling of utter helplessness.

As a part of the TV series the production team sought the advice of a clinical psychologist. The expert, Dr Mair Edwards, explained that we are all afraid of something.

That meant I was in good company. We all, she maintained, as we go through life express the thought, 'I would rather not do this or that.' Or we may think, 'I don't think I'd like to be in that situation.' But we still persevere with our life. That means that the fear has not deteriorated into a phobia. With a phobia, she explained, the fear reaches the point where it stops us from doing something we feel we would like to do eventually. A phobia could even stop us from proceeding with our normal life, our career. I knew that my aversion to water didn't go that far. But, as I said, the fear had always been there at the back of my mind.

There has never been much love lost between me and water. I have experienced some traumatic watery experiences; once in a canoe, and then in a coracle while filming *Cefn Gwlad*. The canoeing experience on Llyn Padarn, and then on Llyn Gwynant in particular, was frightening. I felt as if I was sitting in a giant eggshell. It wobbled at the slightest touch. I was even afraid to breathe in case I capsized. And, if I did, that would be trouble because I couldn't swim.

According to the psychologist, anyone who has a tendency towards a phobia is likely to have more than one. That was true in my case. As well as cats and water I also have a fear of heights and darkness. And although I'm willing to try anything, I do worry beforehand.

As a child I would often go with friends up to Mynydd Bach to bathe in Llyn Eiddwen lake. This was an area where we also herded sheep. We would cycle up there and feel just as privileged as town children with their tiled swimming pools. This cold mountain lake was our swimming pool.

I was constantly warned by Uncle and Aunty to keep away from the lake. They had reason to worry as there had been fatalities there and at nearby Llyn Fanod over the years. In fact, I knew one or two who had drowned there. These thoughts did manage to frighten me, but I still went.

I had made attempts to swim in the past. I would take my son John and some of his friends to Llyn Eiddwen. I always took with me a tractor's inflated inner tube. But on one occasion I slipped through the tube and had to be rescued. Today, with my potbelly, I would be perfectly safe! I would be stuck like a cork in a bottle.

This upcoming challenge would be my second attempt at learning to swim. Back in 1989, I had been filmed in the swimming pool with pupils from Cwm Gwaun Primary School in Pembrokeshire. Those children swam like dolphins. And how they laughed at me with my plastic armbands!

In 2007, almost 20 years later, my granddaughter challenged me to learn to swim. Celine was almost ten years old and she and her friend Elliw Cefn-coch threw down the gauntlet. Initially I decided to be taught secretly and then surprise them. But no, I was foolish enough to agree to do the challenge on camera. And, as I said, to make things more interesting I was issued with that seven-day deadline.

Before my first lesson the director, on camera, asked the opinion of some of Tregaron's residents about my chances of success. The response was mixed. One remarked that I was too fat to use a safety swimming ring. He was right. My old friend Ifan Tregaron remarked that anything shaped like a barrel should float. So I was, according to him, a safe bet!

The first step was an assessment by Stephen Hughes, the manager of Plascrug Swimming Pool in Aberystwyth. I stood in the shallow end dressed in what I believed were a suitable pair of swimming trunks, not too short, not too long. Very smart. And from Stephen I was given some information that wasn't all that promising: anyone over 50 was probably too old to learn to swim. Today children were taught when they started primary school, and by the time they left secondary school every pupil was expected to be able to manage at least one length of a pool.

I was in now, and up to my knees in water. I slowly approached the deepest end until I was up to my waist. Then I was told to crouch and submerge my shoulders. I had been advised by the psychologist that the only way to conquer a fear was to face it. And here I was, up to my neck in water, trying to do just that. I was also up to my neck in trouble for being stupid enough to accept such a challenge.

Next I was told to cross the pool from side to side. But wading, not swimming! This, said Stephen, was an important step, or rather important steps. Then I was told to grab the rail on the side of the pool, lift my legs and kick. I had to repeat the exercise a few dozen times. Then

Stephen stood behind me, grabbed my legs and started pumping them up and down.

Next I was to crouch low until my face was submerged. This was usually, apparently, a learner's worst fear. I hung on to the rail and dipped my head in like a duck searching for worms in a pond. And lo and behold, it wasn't as bad as I had feared! Success!

I was ready for the challenge. I was now determined to learn to swim. I was convinced that it would be a life-changing experience. But a public swimming pool wasn't the place for that. Too many people would see me. I wouldn't be left alone. I was to be sent somewhere no-one would recognise me. That place was Sharm El Sheikh in Egypt! There I would be in the capable hands of diving and underwater swimming expert, Alun Evans.

I knew that wherever I visited in Egypt it would be much warmer than Llanilar. So it was off to Huw Evans' pharmacy in Tregaron for some sun cream and stomach calming pills, the strongest in the shop. Then I had to cross the road to the doctor's surgery where nurse Sandra Evans had some injections to give me. And that would mean facing another fear. I was scared of needles! But, as I suffered with diabetes, I had no choice. Sandra thought that my learning to swim was a wise decision. Swimming was the best possible exercise for losing weight as there was no bodily stress involved. It was also a good way to reduce my cholesterol level. It was already lowering my sanity level!

The next thing to do was the packing. I looked through the various drawers for underwear and shirts but I decided to take only one pair of trousers. I would buy extra pairs out there. I knew I wouldn't need my umbrella. Olwen was rather sceptical about the whole idea. She couldn't believe that I would succeed. And, as she knows me better than anyone, I tended to agree with her. But I reminded her that I had managed to learn to ski. She had no answer to that!

I had long realised that learning to swim would not be anything like learning lines for a play, or the words and music of a song. But as it was all voluntary, I consoled myself that at least I wouldn't have anything to lose. In fact, I was now confident of learning to swim in three or four days.

We were to fly from Gatwick Airport, the film crew, myself, and my old mate Wil Hafod, who had been my companion when I learnt to ski on the piste back in 1990. Wil, as usual, was late arriving. But when he did he was quite confident that I would succeed. I would repeat my success on the snow in the water this time.

On our first morning in Sharm El Sheikh I was five minutes late meeting my tutor for the week. Fair play, it was just past seven o'clock in the morning. My first task, said Alun, would be to feel comfortable in the water. One consolation was the fact that the water at its deepest in the pool would only be up to my chin. Alun was from Maesteg, an ex-pupil of Rhydfelen School. He and his wife Moira had visited Sharm El Sheikh five years previously and had decided to open their own diving school there.

My first task in the pool was to just relax. I had been forewarned by the psychologist that facing my fear would not be easy. In fact, she had added that I would need to be brave. She was right. But she had also said that doing so under the gaze of the camera would strengthen my resolve. It would help me not to make a fool of myself. But no-one had mentioned that to Wil Hafod. When he saw me in my trunks, he collapsed with laughter.

Alun immediately realised that my big problem was my inability to hold my breath for any length of time. The only way out was for me to wear a snorkel. While I was getting used to my mask, Wil took a stroll along the shore of the Red Sea. But, rather than educating himself by reading a book about the pyramids, he decided to enjoy himself at a water park.

In the pool I put on the snorkel and was instructed on how to breathe through my nose. I got used to that and, unbelievably, I was floating without any help from Alun. I was then issued with flippers for my feet. And the first day ended on a high.

As the Good Book says, there was evening and then there was the morning of the second day. I felt muscles I hadn't previously been aware of pulling like elastic. On that second morning we moved from the pool to the Red Sea. This, apparently, is one of the saltiest seas in the world, almost as salty as the Dead Sea. I had no need to sprinkle salt on my chips that day.

The morning lesson entailed natural breathing. I needed to breathe rhythmically. Timing was important. But I was too impetuous. I felt like a newborn lamb trying to gasp its first breath. Alun then told me to kick my legs backwards. And, Glory Be, I was swimming! With some help, it's true. But I was actually swimming! And even more surprising, I was enjoying it! Even Wil Hafod applauded.

That night we just had to go out to celebrate. My treat was a visit to a club to see a belly dancer. Unfortunately, it was no competition. My belly certainly danced far more than hers. Not that it was in any way surprising. My belly was four times larger than hers. And, as Wil and I enjoyed the show, we were handed a hookah pipe. We inhaled the smoke through water. It wasn't pleasant. It tasted as if I was smoking a pair of cremated sweaty socks! We never discovered what the substance we smoked was. Perhaps it was sweaty socks. The smoke turned my stomach and lingered on my tongue for days. I remembered a story about an old chap from Pembrokeshire who was smoking horse manure at the Smithfield Show. He was puffing away in the food queue when one of the waitresses wrinkled her nose and inquired: 'Is that you smoking that terrible shag tobacco?'

'Yes,' he admitted, 'but it's not shag tobacco, it's Gee-gee Number Two!'

The belly dancer invited Wil and I to dance with her. She was quite a sight but wasn't built for loading bales and cleaning out the cowshed back in Ceredigion. And she didn't have Wellington marks on her legs – never a good sign.

On the morning of the third day Alun took me out to the bay. And I remembered the psychologist's words. She maintained that a short deadline would be better than a long one, as a long deadline would also extend the torture. There I was, flippers on my feet, a buoyancy jacket around my shoulders and the snorkel over my face, a hundred yards from the shore and some 20 feet out of my depth.

To crown the third day Wil and I were invited to ride a camel each. Yes, Wil and I, captains on the ships of the desert. Luckily, I had experienced a camel ride before when I filmed the documentary *Jambo Bwana* in the Maasai Mara in Africa with Ken Williams. There, the camels had arrived and immediately dropped down in front of Ken and I. At first I thought that they were too weak to stand. But no, they had been trained to do so. I was advised to sit between the hump and the creature's neck. It then raised its backside, its front legs still kneeling. Then it stood on its front legs. It was like being on a swing. So this time I was ready for anything on a camel.

The first three days had gone well, far better than expected. But it was the calm before the storm. The fourth day was a disaster. Alun was pleased with my progress regarding the snorkelling but felt that my swimming needed more attention. My timing wasn't as good as he expected. I would open my legs but I'd then forget to close them. I blamed tiredness. I had been out in the desert sand but now

I seemed to be in quicksand. But, as the snorkelling had been successful, Alun allowed me to continue wearing the mask.

The psychologist agreed with me. She too attributed my setback to tiredness. I had pushed my limits too far and this had a negative effect on both mind and body. Cramming so much into the first three days was telling on me. The answer was to relax with a massage.

It was my first experience of massage and, as I was being pummelled and pulled apart, Wil was relaxing in the Egyptian sun reading the *Farmers' Weekly*. Probably the Cairo edition! The masseur then decided to walk all over my back. He then pummelled my shoulders. Then he stuck his elbow into my kidneys and, as if this wasn't enough, Alun joined in, pulling my legs apart. I realised then what a wishbone went through on Christmas Day.

It was time to return to the pool. But I opted out and visited a barber in town with Wil. I asked him to wash the sea salt out of my hair and then give me a trim. Then, without asking me, he started shaving me. I swear he wasn't shaving me at all but rather pulling my bristles out from their roots. He then repeated the treatment, with Wil as victim.

The next day it was back to the task in hand. This time we visited the Ras Muhammad National Park, the location of the only coral reef in the northern hemisphere. Alun and Moira did some diving while Wil and I relaxed in the sun. The previous night I had suffered from a nightmare – I was down in the depths when the snorkel pipe dropped out of my mouth. Alun assured me that if such an event happened, all I needed to do was to push the pipe back in. But he didn't convince me at all. Being 20 feet underwater was not the same as crossing the road in Tregaron. However, it didn't put me off the thought of snorkelling.

Alun couldn't hide his disappointment. After the third day he was confident of my success. He was still hopeful during the morning of the fourth day. Then everything went haywire. I totally lost my breathing rhythm due to my inability to relax. Alun mainly blamed himself for that and believed that this was probably the end of the challenge.

But Alun was determined to have me back in the pool on the sixth morning. I agreed to give it a go, using the snorkel but without the flippers. I then confided to Alun one of my weaknesses: given a challenge I have a tendency to rush at it like a bull at the gate and not think and consider. Having got that off my chest I managed to relax. And I felt like a new man. I allowed myself time to think. I rediscovered the necessary tempo. My legs responded to my thoughts. And Alun, sensing success, drove me on. He was so relentless that I asked him whether he was related in any way to King Herod?

I remembered the psychologist's comments again. When in a situation of having to face your fear, and knowing that you won't be able to avoid it, it is important to have beside you someone you can absolutely depend on. Such a person would be able to convince you that you could make it through. She also maintained that being a part of a group helped, as it created a united front. And, in a group, the last thing you want to do is make a fool of yourself with others watching.

I was only one of two, but I had faith in my companion; I knew I could depend on Alun. I literally took the plunge. And I swam a length of the pool! I was now ready to try the sea again. I was now totally unafraid. I again cast off my flippers but kept the snorkel and its connecting pipe. After all, every car needs an exhaust pipe!

Come the seventh day and I ventured to the sea once more. This time we travelled further north, where the breeze was more brisk and the sea churning in a boiling cauldron. But again I made it. Before we turned in that night, Alun took me back to the pool and taught me a new method of swimming. This was turning my whole body as I pulled my arms through the water. This, apparently, was the crawl. Pulling! Turning! Pulling! Turning! It was a tiring session but Alun bullied me into it – for the very best motive. Yes, I made it, and Alun was more delighted than I was. Not only had I learnt to swim, I had managed also to conquer one of my greatest fears.

The last morning dawned and I felt like death warmed up. Something I had eaten the previous night had not agreed with me. I was as sick as a dog. I couldn't even dip my toes in the pool. We were all bitterly disappointed. But I could console myself that I had exceeded all expectations. At the end of the filming Cleif, the director, asked me to

Formal portrait. I must have my shepherd's crook around at all times.

John, with his favourite dog, Bob.

With my favourite dogs, Roy and Craig.

Berthlwyd's stock bull, Iwrch Limited Edition.

An animal from the Nantrhys herd.

Holiday friends feasting! One of my greatest pleasures!

In Ireland filming one of the *Rasus* programmes.

With me dear friend, Trebor Edwards, at the Royal Welsh Show.

Accepting the FUW Cup for my contribution to farming. I received a similar cup from the NFU.

With David Gravell, whose company provided a car for us to travel around the country filming *Cefn Gwlad* for five years.

Photographs of members of Llanilar Young Farmers' Club in the 1980s.

Members of Llanilar Young Farmers' Club after winning the County Rally, a feat achieved five times.

Young Farmers of the Year: John George and Richard Tudor.

Ann Evans (Tudor by now), Ceredigion Young Farmers' Club Queen in 1993.

Wyn Evans, current President of the Livestock Committee, NFU Wales.

Members of Llanilar Young Farmers' Club who won the Welsh Public Speaking under-26 competition. L–R: Alwyn Davies, Gareth Davies, Ann Tudor, Hugh Tudor (former County president).

Members of the cast of *The Practice* in 1979.

Olwen with Sheila Brennan, Young Farmers' County Queen, and John Betws, Young Farmer of the Year.

Being honoured during the year I was president of the Royal Welsh Show in Llanelwedd.

Another memory from the 2010 Royal Welsh when I was president.

Enjoying the 2010 show with Olwen. Being president of the Cardis' Show was one of the greatest honours of my life.

A big moment – holding my BAFTA Cymru Fellowship award.

Being accepted as a Fellow of Aberystwyth University, in the company of Lord Elystan Morgan and Derec Llwyd Morgan.

DAI JONES

Ehedodd gyda'r adar-a hedeg
drwy'r wlad gyda'i drydar,
hwn Frenin ein gwerin gwâr,
llawn o hwyl yw Llanilar.

A poem by Tudur Dylan Jones which will grace my headstone.

Wearing my mortar board after accepting an honour for my contribution to the stage and agriculture.

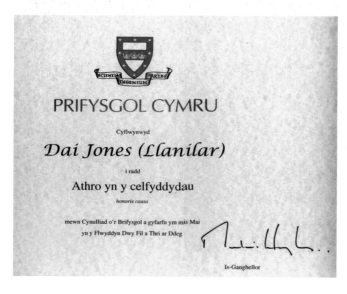

PRIFYSGOL CYMRU

Cyflwynwyd

Dai Jones (Llanilar)

i radd

Athro yn y celfyddydau

honoris causa

mewn Cynulliad o'r Brifysgol a gyfarfu ym mis Mai
yn y Flwyddyn Dwy Fil a Thri ar Ddeg

Is-Ganghellor

My Masters of Arts certificate from the University of Wales, 2013.

With Olwen after accepting the MBE.

The ever-loyal *Cefn Gwlad* film crew.

come up with an appropriate closing quip. I was standing on the shore of the Red Sea and all I could say was, 'Moses, where were you when I needed you?'

I had conquered one of my fears and was ready to surprise Celine and Elliw at the pool in Aberystwyth. I arrived there before them and insisted that I needed a snorkel and the flippers. And when Celine arrived, her 'dad-cu' jumped in and swam with her and Elliw. I even challenged them to a race. I was the only swimmer wearing a snorkel and flippers, but I was swimming!

I still fear cats, heights, darkness and injections, but I am now completely happy in water. I went through hell and the Red Sea on my way there, but I made it. And I discovered that learning to swim is exactly like learning to ride a bike. Once you learn how to do it, you will never lose your ability to do so. I can still swim, provided I can wear my mask and flippers. Sometimes I have a dip in the river, making sure the bank isn't too far away. Well, nobody's perfect.

In Egypt I learnt something else also. I discovered the reason why Moses had to part the Red Sea to escape from the Pharaoh. For one thing, Moses couldn't swim. But there was another reason; he had left his Wellington boots at home.

10

A man for all seasons

CEFN GWLAD HAS now been running without a break for three decades. That means we have produced hundreds of episodes. One question I am often asked is whether I have a personal favourite from among them all. When I am asked that question I am reminded of singer Meic Stevens being asked to choose his favourite personal composition. He answered by saying that he looked on all his songs as he would his children: he loved every one. And that's how I feel.

Yet, if I was pressed to make a choice, I would be tempted to choose the documentary which followed the footsteps of a quite remarkable man. He was Don Garreg Ddu who farmed some three miles from Llanrhaeadr-ym-Mochnant in Denbighshire. I filmed Don and his family on three occasions. The first is mentioned in my earlier autobiography, *Dai and Let Live*. The success of that first documentary meant return visits in 1989 and in 1996.

Don Morris and his wife Eunice lived at Garreg Ddu, meaning 'Black Boulder'. They farmed there with their two sons, Richard and Dei, but known to one and all as Dico and Bando. They had another son and daughter but they had flown the nest. Alas, both Don and Eunice are no longer with us but Dico and Bando remain. Dico has built a new house on Garreg Ddu land, while Bando lives in the village.

Some of you will remember various highlights from the first documentary. The programme was based on Don primarily; he was a true son of the soil who still adhered to the old Welsh way of life and work. We watched Don clearing the lane of loose stones and loading them onto a sled-like cart on runners drawn by Bess, his faithful 12-year-old mare. Don could recall as many as six horses at a time being kept at Garreg Ddu.

We then showed him carrying loads of cow manure, and him dumping small heaps of it every six yards to be spread later. He was filmed ploughing the slopes using a one-ridge plough – Bess hauling away and Don between the plough handles. He could be heard coaxing and cajoling the faithful old mare, 'Ty'd 'mlaen, Bess fach!' And Bess reacting and drawing the plough along like a knife through butter. And the irony of it all as we filmed that day: the tractor refused to start, so Bess had to give it a tow before the engine fired. One horse power dragging a 50-horsepower tractor! There is a modern parable there somewhere.

It was there on the high slopes that Don was in his element. He wouldn't change places with a king. In the house, over a cup of tea, he recalled how he and Eunice had first met at a local concert in Llanrhaeadr. He then spoke of his other two loves, hunting and watching wrestling. I look back on that documentary with both love and pride. No wonder it was awarded a prize at the Pan Celtic Festival in Killarney the following year.

We returned in 1989 to film a Christmas special. This time we wanted to portray how Garreg Ddu farm faced all four seasons, beginning in deep winter with snow on the ground. We opened the programme again with Don and Bess, the old mare this time carrying two sacks full of feed for the sheep on the surrounding hills. Bess was expecting a foal in early May. Don reminisced about the rodeo that used to be a part of the local agricultural show where he had enjoyed considerable success.

We suddenly received a call from a neighbour. A vixen had been spotted killing lambs. Off we went with Don's dogs, and he and the boys were armed with shotguns. On the way we saw the mutilated corpse of a newborn lamb. We found the fox's warren and Don sent in his two terriers. He was kneeling above one of the foxholes when suddenly he swooped down and brought out a young vixen by its neck.

Bess duly gave birth to a foal in May. It was named Duke. Bess was soon back in harness dragging logs. A local poet had written a poem in praise of Don. One verse went:

I fyny'r garn mewn harnes
Yn fore llafuria hyd heuldes,
Dyna bâr yw Don a Bess,
Rhai hydrin a dirodres.

(Along the ridge in harness
From morning until darkness,
What a pair are Don and Bess,
So active and so selfless.)

Bess dragged the logs up the slopes without any problem, while I was reduced to crawling on my hands and knees. We then filmed calves being tagged before they were turned out to graze. Don recalled the time when he grew and harvested oats. Threshing day sometimes overran to two days. Then it was off to the bracken stack to cut a bundle that would be used as bedding for Bess. We later filmed the sheep being marked with a red 'M' on their backs and having their ears snipped to denote that they were Garreg Ddu sheep. A cut was made to the tip of the right ear, and a stump marked under the left.

To Don's delight we attended a wrestling match at the village hall one night. Don was so worked up that he jumped into the ring to help a wrestler he felt was being ill-treated. Don was a champion of fair play.

One of the hardest farm tasks was carting hay in a sled pulled by Bess. The cart was just a flat pallet with props on each corner. I helped Don and Eunice with the loading. We followed Bess and her heavy load to the stackyard, with Don testifying that he had never once failed to bring in the hay. He rued the loss of the old ways that he still favoured. Neighbours didn't come to each others' aid today, he said. It was everyone for himself. We then filmed a sad occasion for Don – the last ever market in Llanrhaeadr, bringing to an end centuries of tradition.

The next task we filmed was Don cutting bracken with a scythe. He recalled the days when he worked as a young farmhand, earning £2.10s. a week. We discussed the demise of old dialects and compared notes on the differences between my dialect and his. And then Don recalled his and Eunice's last holiday. It was their honeymoon, when they had spent two days in Liverpool. Was there anywhere special he would like to visit? Yes, he would quite like to spend a week in Australia. A week? It would have taken him almost a whole day to reach there!

We just had time enough to do some drainage work before making it to Seion chapel's harvest festival. Don's neighbour, Gwilym Jones, Tŷ Cerrig, offered a prayer, and the minister, the Rev. Raymond Hughes, welcomed members of the congregation from the valley and the surrounding hills to join in thanks.

When we filmed the third documentary at Garreg Ddu in 1996, we concentrated on the sons, Dico and Bando. As I arrived they met me on the farmyard with their dozen or more dogs: sheepdogs, terriers and even a greyhound or two. The sheep had all been penned for shearing, and I swear there were as many dogs as there were sheep. The whole pack was running and jumping around as if possessed!

The brothers would take the dogs for a stroll every evening and each one had a name. How the lads remembered those names, I don't know. There was a Siwsi and a Jiwdi and a Joci among them, as well as some names that were more imaginative, such as Dŵli and Hovis. And then there was a Toohey, named after Tooheys, a brand of New Zealand beer. And for some unknown reason, one dog was named Bobby Robson!

Eunice was busy feeding the motherless lambs, while Dico was shearing the last of the sheep. Bando was wrapping the fleeces. Dico felt that farmers were shearing their sheep far too early nowadays. But following unseasonably warm weather, the sheep must have been glad to be able to shed their wool. Most farmers held their shearing day around the middle of May.

Dico, for 11 years in succession, spent the shearing season out in New Zealand. He could recall every mile he had travelled on his first visit. He accompanied a friend from Beddgelert who had been out there once previously. It was quite an adventure for a home-loving countryman like Dico. He said initially that he would shear only around 200 sheep a day. Only around 200? I hadn't sheared that many during my lifetime! But, according to Dico, a seasoned shearer was expected to shear some 300 sheep a day in New Zealand.

Dico's car was a revelation. It was virtually a skip on four wheels. It was chock-a-block with shearing equipment. The back seat resembled a ransacked office, piled with papers, magazines and all kinds of rubbish. Among the flotsam was a poster advertising Corwen Shears and that was stuck on one of the windows. On the Ford's passenger seat was a sleeping bag, a pair of pyjamas and a leather bag full of documents. The car was a bedroom and an office all-in-one. It was, said Dico, very handy for courting purposes as well. But my question was, where could his girlfriend find any room? Only God, Dico and his girlfriend knew that answer.

It was good to see a reminder of my previous visits. Bess the mare was still the queen of Garreg Ddu's animals. As Bando led her across the yard, she was followed by her latest foal. Dico put a bridle around the foal's head. She wasn't happy and began kicking and jumping around. She then planted her front hooves in the ground and refused to move. Although only two months old, she stubbornly refused to budge. She was anchored to the yard. It became a tug-of-war between her and Dico. I had to give Dico a helping hand before she moved. But she soon allowed me to stroke her muzzle. It would only be a matter of time before she succumbed to regular human contact. She would be needed for work on the farm before very long. Her mother was ageing and the foal had been earmarked to replace her. Don knew more than anyone that Bess' days were numbered.

Don, however, was as active as ever. When I arrived he was sawing logs. Not that he needed any. The warmth of Garreg Ddu didn't emanate from the roaring fire on the hearth. Rather, it radiated from the hearts of the family that lived there. I looked at Don's massive hands. They were as big as shovels and accustomed to toil.

We adjourned to the house and sat in the front parlour for a chat. Bando recalled his success as a long-distance runner. At one time the local community would hold an annual nine-mile race. Dico, at his first attempt, was just pipped to first place. He was beaten over the line by his brother Tom. But on the mantelpiece there were trophies that were evidence of Dico's later successes.

Garreg Ddu stood over two miles from the chapel and the boys remembered walking there across the fields every Sunday morning. Then they would eat dinner with friends in the village before returning for the afternoon service. Don was a chapel deacon. Bando didn't quite see himself emulating his father by being appointed deacon also.

Unlike his brother Dico, Bando wasn't one for travelling abroad. He had no wish to travel further than Scotland to see how his Celtic cousins farmed. At home his only real interest now, besides his work, was hunting.

Dico had been an accomplished darts player and had played regularly for the Hand Inn in the village. This had meant playing in a league consisting of pub teams from Llangynog, Pen-y-bont-fawr and Llansanffraid. Unfortunately, there was little to attract young people in the area on a Saturday night. The custom now was for a crew of youngsters to hire a minibus to take them to either Oswestry or over the Berwyn mountains to Bala.

Now with the shearing season all but over, what would there be to amuse the brothers? High on the agenda would be attending village agricultural shows leading up to the main event, the Royal Welsh Show at Llanelwedd. There were also a few greyhound or terrier races here and there, and the brothers would enter some of their menagerie of dogs. But would Dico go to New Zealand for the coming shearing season? He hadn't yet decided. Having skipped two successive seasons he would like to go. But there was work to be done at home.

In came Don carrying a bundle of logs to make the hearth even warmer. But we decided to wander out to the far end of the yard where there was a collection of decrepit old cars. Indeed, it resembled a cemetery for vehicles. Dico led me from one to the other, every car in turn having its own story. There was his brother Tom's old car, about the only banger that seemed to be close to working order. It had been driven by Dico until he was offered his present car for £100. Tom's car was now full of firewood. But under the passenger seat, for some unknown reason, was a pair of yellow shoes. The vehicle cemetery wasn't just confined to cars – among them were rusty old tractors and farm implements too.

Unexpectedly, the sun broke through the clouds giving Dico the opportunity to load the spreader with cow manure. It was attached to a brand-new tractor, a yellow Renault. Quite a change from Bess and her rickety old cart. Bando had seen fit to disappear while his brother loaded the trailer.

It was now a beautifully sunny day with a slight breeze blowing from the Berwyn mountains. There we were, on a hill some 1,500 feet above sea level. Like heaven, it wasn't an easy place to reach but it was well worth the bother of getting there. There wasn't a spare pitchfork around, but Dico, seeing that his brother had disappeared, handed me Bando's fork. So I pitched in with him.

With the muck spreader filled, Bando returned just in time to drive the tractor. Dico spoke of his father's total disinterest in tractors. Only Bess would do. The brothers put their faith in four wheels; Don in four legs.

Back on the farmyard the dogs were playing whatever it was that dogs play. The boys decided to go for a drive. As soon as they opened the car doors, some half-dozen dogs jumped in. One of them joined me in the front passenger seat. The rest joined Bando on the back seat. Off we went and following us was a terrier that hadn't been able to make it into the car in time. I felt as if I was in Noah's Ark! But this ark was exclusive to dogs. By now one dog was sitting in Dico's lap in the driving seat, its head poking out through the open window and trying to catch the wind in its mouth.

We were on our way to catch rabbits in Llanrhaeadr. We parked beneath the famous falls that gave the village its name, 'rhaeadr' meaning 'waterfall'. As soon as we stopped the car the dogs leapt out of the open windows and we had to run to catch up with them. They ran straight through the river, up the slopes, through the bracken, and we tried to follow them. A rabbit shot out of its hiding place and the yelping dogs leapt over the fence in pursuit. The rabbit got away but we climbed higher and higher through the pine trees towards the head of the falls.

It had been quite a climb but, according to Dico, descending would be even harder. In fact, the climb had been so steep that, on occasions, I had been forced to use my hands to grab the undergrowth to help pull myself up. Even the dogs found it difficult, especially the short-legged terriers. I had to rest for a while so that I could catch my breath. That gave us all a respite and even the dogs were pleased.

We then resumed and, at long last, reached the top of the waterfall. The dogs' tongues were hanging out and they lapped the cool, clear water on the summit. And what a view from the top! I was looking at one of the wonders of Wales, indeed the world. Way down below, the newly-arrived visitors looked like ants. The waterfall dropped down vertically from virtually under our feet and the noise of the falling water was deafening.

Yes, the Pistyll Rhaeadr is one of the wonders of nature and attracts thousands of people every year. That day the visitor centre held a shearing exhibition. But we had better things to do, starting with downing a well deserved pint each. To the lads, climbing up to the top of the falls was something that they did every Saturday as a means of exercising the dogs. To me it had been my first time – and my last if I could help it!

Back we went to Garreg Ddu where it was a case of déjà vu. During my first visit we had a riotous time trying to catch a wild young stallion. And now we were to do something similar. The gray mare, Bess' daughter, had given birth to a colt that hadn't yet been tamed. Also there was a large blue stallion. Remembering my previous experience, I tried to keep my distance. But the lads loved a challenge. The young stallion was four years old and had never felt a halter around its head. We fitted one over the mother's head without any trouble. But the colt was a different beast. We caught him quite easily, but as we walked him down the lane he got stubborn, leaping around and kicking out. Dico asked me to tie a rope around its head. I was cagey, remembering my previous escapade. Bando, however, had a special gift and the young colt allowed him to stroke its nose. I wondered whether he used the same technique with the young ladies of the district! But the colt's obedience didn't last for long. Suddenly, he leapt and kicked out, neighing and stamping his hooves. Bando held on to the rope like a leech. I could imagine the colt dragging him all the way to Pen-y-bont-fawr. Dico was doubtful whether the local girls would rebuff Bando's sweet-talking in such a way! Gradually the young colt succumbed to the feel of the halter.

As well as working at home, Bando helped out at a neighbouring dairy farm. He had originally gone there to help out for a week. But 15 years later he was still there and enjoying every minute. His greatest joy was driving the Massey Ferguson. I joined him on the tractor and we drove over to view a herd of cows.

At a time when neighbouring farmers were complaining about the price of straw, Don had harvested and baled bracken in abundance. He had cut it using the old method of scything. In three weeks' time the bracken would be dry enough to use as bedding for the animals.

Once again I joined the brothers and their dogs in the hope of catching a few rabbits. This time they brought along a ferret as well, a sleek creature named Sam. We stopped at a rabbit warren and Sam was coaxed into a burrow. Immediately a rabbit bolted out, and the dogs took after it, barking furiously. Don tried to persuade me to hold Sam. But to someone who was scared of cats, seeing Sam's sharp little teeth was enough to put me off.

Dico and Bando were now shouting and stamping their feet among the rushes, their histrionics disturbing rabbits and causing them to bolt and, in turn, attract the attention of the dogs. They never caught a single rabbit but did manage to catch a fine hare.

That evening we attended a dog race meeting in Llanrhaeadr. The dogs were asked to chase an artificial hare, or rather a fox tail tied to a long rope wound around the rim of a wheel. I was given the honour of operating the device. The Garreg Ddu dogs gave a good account of themselves, the brothers urging them on with calls of 'Hw! Hw!'.

To end an enjoyable evening we called in at the local pub for a pint and a sing-song. And to make it an even better occasion there was wrestling on the TV. Some young men find amusement in the towns and cities. The Garreg Ddu lads were true sons of the Berwyn mountains, and how I enjoyed their company.

*

I am often reminded of my visits to Garreg Ddu. I will never forget that first visit and the saga of catching the stallion. We struggled to coax and drag him along the farmyard and into the shed. There he stood on his hind legs, with his head literally raising the roof. He then kicked a yellow plastic bucket high in the air. I'm minded to believe that it is still up there somewhere in orbit. After we managed to restrain the creature with a halter, I was daft enough to hold the end of the rope. The stallion dragged me head-first out of the shed and into a ditch!

Then there was the occasion when we were in Dico's Fiesta surrounded by a dozen excitable dogs. I opened my side window to get some fresh air. A rabbit ran across the road and the dogs, like the Gadarene Swine, jumped over me and out through the window. I have heard of the Hounds of Hell. The Garreg Ddu dogs would have torn them apart.

Then there was the unforgettable night when Bando celebrated his birthday in the Three Tuns Inn. His mates had secretly hired a stripogram to surprise him. She was dressed as a policewoman. Afterwards he went around telling everyone he met that he had been given a radiogram on his birthday!

I will never forget the very first time I met Don Garreg Ddu. It was a dull, drizzly old day. And he came to meet me through the mist, a sack draped loosely over his broad shoulders. I could well have been looking at my own grandfather. And then the firm handshake, with my hand disappearing completely into his massive hand as he pressed it over mine.

Meeting Don Garreg Ddu and his family was a rare privilege. They don't make men like Don any more. Unforgettable!

11

Where the heart is

WHEN A POET honours you with a verse, you have attained one of two stations. You have either achieved something of note or you have just died. I don't believe the latter applies to me. Not yet anyway! But I have been the subject of numerous poems, most of them complimentary. I must mention one in particular. It is the verse that will be written on my gravestone after I die.

Ehedoddodd gyda'r adar – a hedeg
   drwy'r wlad gyda'i drydar,
  hwn, frenin ein gwerin gwâr,
  llawn o hwyl yw Llanilar.

The gist of it means: 'He flew with the birds, flitting through the land with his singing, he, king of the civilised common people, full of spirit is Llanilar.' The place name Llanilar is always coupled with my name. It is always 'Dai Llanilar'. The *englyn* was composed by Tudur Dylan Jones, and commissioned by a friend, television director Gareth Vaughan Jones, as a present for my 70th birthday. Gareth helps produce a farming series on S4C and is the son of

Meirion Jones, founder and conductor of the Brythoniaid Male Voice Choir.

The past 20 years have been a pleasure interspersed here and there with a few setbacks. Unfortunately, 2015 was a traumatic year for my granddaughter Celine, as it was for the whole family. In May she was rehearsing with Llanddewibrefi's Young Farmers' Club for the tug-of-war competition that was to be held at the County Rally, when she suddenly felt a lump in her neck. She went to the doctor and was immediately sent to see a specialist in Carmarthen. She was given a scan and it showed that she was suffering with lymphatic cancer.

I will never forget the moment when I heard the news. I arrived home from filming and Olwen was waiting for me at the door. I immediately realised from her expression that something was wrong. And then she told me without any preamble, 'I've got some bad news for you, Dai. Celine has cancer.'

Hearing the dreaded word 'cancer' was enough in itself. I felt as if someone had pierced my heart with a corkscrew. I was halfway out of the car when I heard the news. It took me a good quarter of an hour before I could move any further. I was stunned. But providence is a strange thing. There I was, sitting at the kitchen table sipping tea, still numbed by the news, when a neighbour's brother happened to call. He was Patrick Loxdale, a surgeon in Plymouth. His brother lived nearby at Castle Hill. He realised immediately that there was something wrong. We explained the situation and he told us that lymphatic cancer was one of the least dangerous cancers and that it was eminently treatable. And Patrick talked us through everything. He gave us hope. Never had a cup of tea suddenly tasted so sweet. In a matter of seconds it turned from wormwood to honey.

Yes, we were much relieved but naturally still very worried. The lowest moment came when Olwen went with Celine to Aberystwyth to help her choose a wig. It was expected that one of the side effects of treatment would be her hair falling out. Fortunately that did not happen. Not only did she retain her hair, she also retained her spirit.

The news regarding Celine's condition spread quickly. And that was when Olwen and I realised how numerous and how true our friends were. We received messages from all over Wales and well beyond. People called round, telephoned, and wrote to us offering sympathy and support. Every message strengthened us. Celine was told she would need 12 sessions of chemotherapy as part of her treatment. Her resolve never wavered. When our shearing day arrived, she was out there helping with the fleeces.

She had been accepted on a teachers' training course, specialising in nursery children, at the University of Wales Trinity St David based in Carmarthen and Lampeter. She requested that she study at home while receiving her treatment. Sadly her request was refused. She was told that the only alternative would be for her to postpone her training for a year. However, Aberystwyth University was contacted and she was allowed to join the appropriate course there and study at home until her treatment was over. She had already spent six months as a student teacher at Llangeitho Primary School and had loved every minute of it there.

Fortunately, she needed only five of the planned 12 chemotherapy sessions, followed by radiotherapy in Swansea. She fully recovered, much to our relief. She was soon back following her course and helping us on the farm during her spare time. Her little sister Ella was so protective of Celine. One day, Ella was out with me as I injected a sheep. She asked me: 'Will that make the sheep better?'

'Yes,' I answered, 'much better.'

She retorted innocently, 'Why can't you inject Celine as well and make her better?'

*

During Celine's illness, my way of getting by was to immerse myself in my work, both at home and in the media. I find it hard to comprehend that my media work started as far back as 1966, which means that I have been involved in that industry almost continuously now for over 50 years. I began with the occasional job. Then came my big break with *Siôn a Siân*, the Welsh version of the family quiz show *Mr and Mrs*. I was appointed initially for six months. But I ended up presenting it for 17 years.

One of the successes of the show was its scheduling. It was televised at supper time on Saturday nights, allowing viewers time afterwards to go out for a drink. I worked with quite a few co-presenters. You could say that I had more co-presenters than Henry VIII had wives! I am, however, remembered chiefly for my partnership with Jenny Ogwen. Three years ago the show celebrated its 50th anniversary with a special programme filmed at the Pontrhydfendigaid Pavilion. Jen and I were brought back together, as was the original piano accompanist on the show, Janice Ball. We were back together as a threesome for the first time since the mid 1970s. Janice was an important member of the team, as I would sing a song on every show and needed an accompanist.

The star of the anniversary show was Clive Rowlands, who was accompanied by his wife Marged. I'm a great admirer of Clive. He has contributed immensely to Wales, not only through rugby but also as a supporter of all that is good in Welsh life. His bubbly sense of humour is unique. And as for *Siôn a Siân*, I am confident that it will go on to celebrate its centenary.

I also presented *Rasus* for 20 years, a programme that followed trotting meetings all over Wales and beyond. *Cefn Gwlad*, of course, has run for over 30 years. And I can't even remember when I started fronting my Sunday night radio request programme, *Ar Eich Cais*, on Radio Cymru.

I have witnessed many changes, not all of them changes for the better. Many characters that starred in various episodes of *Cefn Gwlad* have left us now. Among them are Don Garreg Ddu, Joni Moch and Meri Pantafon. It would be banal to say that we will never see their likes again. But banal or not, it is also partly true. No, we will never see their likes, but we will – indeed we are – still encountering characters. But they are different characters. They are not as numerous as they used to be. But they are there all the same.

Cefn Gwlad today tends to concentrate more on people's activities than on their personalities. Today, what people do is more interesting than who they are. People are more stereotyped these days. There are more types than individuals. Everyone seems to follow the same life pattern, meaning that there are fewer people who are deemed to be 'different'. But they are there if you look for them.

I believe it is important for us to continue showing the world what country life is all about, what agriculture really contributes. Unfortunately, fewer and fewer young people are attracted to farming today. And who can blame them? By the time they reach 18 years of age, more and more of them go on to further education – which is great thing, of course. Sadly, we then lose them. I fear for the future of farming during the next decade. In the past, Labour governments were condemned by many for nationalising everything. Today nationalisation happens without us realising it. It comes in through the back door.

Here in the Ystwyth valley we have a farming community that is doing its best. But we are continually plagued by bureaucratic busybodies who bombard us with meaningless questions. How much meat can we produce? How can we produce more? I'm afraid that what we produce mostly these days is dung, slurry... and more bureaucrats.

I feel that the Government over the past few years has been shameless in its attitude towards farmers. I have already referred to the emphasis on diversification. I have been lucky enough in that I have been able to diversify by working in the media for the past 50 years. Not all farmers have been so lucky. To me it has been vital. It is what has spread a little jam on my bread and butter.

Then the Government urges us farmers to diversify further. We already have. We already work seven days a week. Now we are expected to diversify what we've already diversified!

In this part of the world many young women, farmers' wives and daughters, have to find alternative work. Many are teachers. This is a great help in keeping the wolf from the door. It isn't often that I feel depressed. I am a natural optimist, but it hurts to see how the Government and organisations like DEFRA treat farmers. These politicians and bureaucrats have no idea of the real situation. They put agriculture through hell and lecture us about what to do and treat us like naughty little children.

Diversification today comes at a heavy price. Take contract work, something we do on the farm here. If you buy a new tractor you won't get much change from £100,000. And for silage work you need two or three of them. Whatever device a tractor tows is likely to cost you another £30,000 or so, such as a hay tedder for aerating hay, or a hay rake for collecting hay in windrows. Then there's the need for a baler, and you need a driver for each tractor. Then there's the cost of stacking bales. You could say that the process involves seven stages and the total cost can be enormous.

Thank goodness for the occasional distraction. My favourite diversion is the Royal Welsh Show. To me that means a week of presenting on S4C. It is work, yes, but it also brings me total satisfaction. I would go as far as to say that the show is now my life. It lasts less than a week but it takes months of preparation.

The Royal Welsh Show is administered by the most efficient crew I have ever known, be it the chief administrator, chairs of the various departments – everyone, on all levels. Attending the various meetings is a pleasure and most of the time there will be total agreement. When there isn't, there will be a good reason for it. It won't be discord just for the sake of it. Should there be a disagreement, it will be a constructive one.

The Royal Welsh Show Society is central to Welsh agricultural life. The show itself has been televised in Wales for years and now, thanks to satellite television, it can be seen worldwide. In fact, we are the subject of no little envy due to all the various television programmes which has the countryside at centre stage.

One of my greatest pleasures nowadays is attending and competing at sheepdog trials. I hope to do more of these in the future. I remember my first sheepdog, a present from my uncle who lived at Brynchwith. It cost him five pounds. I had just returned home from school and was having my tea when I felt something running around my legs beneath the table. Back then, sheepdogs would not be allowed in the house. Then I was told that the dog was my birthday present.

With my uncle's help I trained him. And I started competing in local trials. As I grew more confident I started competing at a wider level. I remember running a dog in Gwenlli, near New Quay. The trials were held on the same day and at the same venue as the annual sports. My name was announced as 'Dai Jones *Siôn a Siân*'. There was an immediate response. All those watching the sports rushed over to watch the sheepdog trials. I have never in my life felt so nervous. My dog was called Moss. I tried to send him to the right with a call of 'Away!' Moss ran the opposite way and jumped in through the open window of the car where the judge and his clerk were sitting. Moss landed among them! All I could see was a shower of papers flying around the car's interior. I gradually improved however, and later I went on to win a place in the Wales team competing out in Ireland. At present I have two promising dogs. My ambition is that one day I will be chosen to captain the Wales team.

The sheepdog trials season usually starts around Easter time. One of the first meetings is at Bodfari in Denbighshire on Easter Saturday. Competitors come from as far away as Cumbria. Thanks to the superior condition of roads across the border, they make the journey in better time than I can, even though I'm only travelling from Llanilar. In Bodfari I can see growing pasture for the first time that year. But here in Llanilar there isn't any pasture worth mentioning yet. I would see more growing grassland in the Clwyd Valley at Easter than I would see here, even in July!

Fortunately for me, farming and the media overlap. In both, the countryside is central. And these days Olwen will take over the driving – especially if we need to reverse – allowing me to see and enjoy even more of it. This allows me the chance to appreciate the good work of other farmers in different parts of Wales.

And on the subject of Olwen, she deserves a medal – a long service medal at that – for being far more than my wife. She has been my support over the years. I was only 23 when we married. Olwen was even younger. We first met at a cattle judging competition organised by the Young Farmers' Clubs Federation in Crosswood. She has been my prop, someone to lean on, ever since. And as I was away so often, I could never have coped without her. She took over the farm duties, bringing in the cows and milking them. She would take care of the lambing. And should someone call, Olwen would be there to greet them and often feed them royally. Last year we celebrated our golden wedding anniversary. Nothing grand, just a night out with the family.

We were married on 22 October 1966, the day after the Aberfan disaster. We left for our honeymoon in an Austin 1100 following the reception at the Marine Hotel in

Aberystwyth. We drove away from the promenade with no plans as to where to go. Our honeymoon was a mystery trip, a mystery even to us. We didn't even know whether to head north or south. We decided on the north, ending up in Lockerbie in Scotland. From there we headed back south to the Dairy Show in London. But then I received a phone call informing me that one of the cows had died. Its stomach had swollen after eating too much rapeseed. I still remember the cow's name. It was Duchess. And I had to drive my own duchess back home prematurely.

Olwen and I had a long courtship before we decided to marry. Like every young couple back then we tried for a while to hide the fact that we were seeing one another. It's different today. A young couple nowadays will meet in town on a Saturday night and will be at the new partner's parents' house drinking tea by Monday. I am old-fashioned in such things. I believe that a year should go by before the boyfriend or girlfriend is introduced to the sweetheart's family. Back in the 1960s, should a young couple be seen walking together into a public function in the local hall, the audience would clap and shout. What an embarrassment that would be! Many young couples would therefore do their courting in private until they felt they could safely appear in public. Talk about coming out!

There was an element of respect too, I feel, in keeping the relationship a secret for a while. And I am a great believer in such conduct. Respect is all-important to me, especially from children towards their parents. With our son John, his grandfather, Olwen's father, was the great influence. He lived nearby and was John's hero. John has always addressed me as 'Dai'. We are on excellent terms, more like brothers than father and son.

I have mentioned before the privileges I have enjoyed. It was a privilege to be raised in Llangwrddon among some great characters, characters that I would revere. Take the Felin boys, Joe and Steven, or 'Styfin' to us. They were the greatest spitters ever born. Should you set up a target at the far end of the farmyard, the Felin brothers would hit it every time. They could have won medals for Wales for chewing Ringer's tobacco and their accuracy in spitting.

Then there was Wil Woodward. His shop was the local debating chamber. It was Llangwrddon's House of Commons. Wil, with his ever-present Craven "A" cigarette forever dangling from his lips, and I sitting on an upturned apple box listening to the words of wisdom uttered by Wil and Ifan Williams, Rhandir Uchaf; Dewi Jones, Ffynnonwen; Dafydd Thomas, Y Felin; Tom Davies, Penglanowen, and William Evans, Tanglogau. These were the sages of the community. And then Ned, Y Llain, joker and leg-puller, who was always in his element with children. Dic the Blacksmith, postman; Edwin James, carpenter; Lisi Pengelli and her brother, Owen, who kept Speckled Face sheep. And Mari Langors, who always clicked her tongue, making you think there was an electric fence nearby. There is a central African tribe who communicate through